# Tell us a story

## Stories and outlines for infant assemblies

**Annie Brown**

**Scripture Union**
130 City Road, London EC1V 2NJ

*To Mary Fooks – Vice-principal (retired) of Newton Park College, Avon – a dedicated teacher.*

Grateful thanks to the headmistress, staff, parents and children of Redfield Edge Primary School, Oldland Common, Bristol for their interest, encouragement and support.

**British Library Cataloguing in Publication Data**
Brown, Annie
Tell us a story: Stories and outlines for infant assemblies.
1. Infant schools. Morning assembly. Themes
I. Title
377.14

ISBN 0–86201–576–6



First published 1990

ISBN 0–86201–576–6



Design: Sue Ainley

Phototypeset by Input Typesetting Ltd, London

Printed and bound in Great Britain by Cox and Wyman Ltd, Reading

# Contents

# Introduction

This material has been chosen to introduce young children to some familiar stories from the Bible that can be linked with their own experience.

The family theme is used to help children become aware of their place in the family of Christ. The children are encouraged to find out about their environment and to explore their relationships with others, within a framework of Christian values.

Some related poems, prayers, songs and stories have been included so that teachers can select those most appropriate to their needs. Teachers with limited resources can find the books suggested for further reading in County Library collections.

There are stories for Christian festivals, and for particular times of the year, whilst others can be used at any time. Each story can be read in isolation, or used as a starting point for classroom activities. Children could be prepared to read their own written work, display models and pictures, make music or present a play. Only brief suggestions for follow-up work have been included since most teachers prefer to work from children's interest.

ASSEMBLY 1

# The party

## (The parable of the ungrateful friends)

*Luke 14:16–24*

---

This Assembly introduces one of the parables Jesus told, about ungrateful friends, and giving to those who truly appreciate the gift. It is also about not giving only when you expect a gift in return.

Further themes that the children can deal with are:
Keeping your word,
Giving, even if you would prefer to keep the gift yourself.

## Hymns and songs

**Take Care of a Friend** (*p35*) Every Colour Under the Sun (*Ward Lock*)
**Jesus I Thank You** (*13*) Come and Sing Some More (*Scripture Union*)

## Read the story

## The party

On the day that Grandma came to visit, Katie was wearing her best party dress. She ran up to Grandma and gave her a kiss.

'You do look beautiful, Katie,' said Grandma.

'Thank you, Grandma,' said Katie, 'Do you like my new shoes?'

'Oh, yes, Katie, they're lovely,' said Grandma.

Grandma looked in her handbag and found the special perfume that she let Katie wear. She sprayed some behind Katie's ears and onto her wrists.

'It's cold,' giggled Katie.

Katie's mum came in from the kitchen where she had been making a cup of tea.

'Katie's going to a party,' she said to Grandma. 'Have you got Rebecca's present, Katie?'

'Yes,' said Katie, holding something behind her back.

'Let me see,' said Mum.

Katie brought out a crumpled parcel. She looked upset.

'That's not the little pony we bought for Rebecca,' said Mum, and Katie began to cry. Mum unwrapped the parcel. It was one of Katie's old colouring books.

'Where's the little pony, Katie?' asked Mum.

Katie didn't answer but just cried louder while Mum looked in the toy cupboard. She soon found the little pony, still in its box. She looked very cross.

'I'm not going to the party,' screamed Katie, 'I don't want to go. I want to stay at home and play with the pony.'

'You certainly will go, my girl,' said Mum. 'We told Rebecca that you were coming and that pony is for her. Her mother will have got food ready for you and you're not going to let her down. I don't know what all the fuss is about, you'll have a lovely time. Now go and wash your face.'

Grandma went upstairs with Katie, who was still crying. They went into the bathroom and Grandma started to comb Katie's shiny brown hair. Katie enjoyed having her hair combed, and started to calm down.

'Don't you like Rebecca?' asked Grandma.

Katie just nodded, and the tears started to run down her cheeks again.

'Why don't you want to go to her party?' asked Grandma.

In between sobs, Katie told Grandma what was the matter.

'Rebecca's got hundreds of ponies and I've only got two. Everyone's going to give her a pony, so she wouldn't miss mine,' she said. 'Anyway, I don't want to go to the party. It won't be any fun. I want to stay at home.'

'Listen, Katie, I'll tell you a story about a party,' said Grandma.

Katie stopped crying then because she always liked Grandma's stories. Grandma carried on combing Katie's hair while she told her the story.

'This is a story that Jesus told,' said Grandma.

'The baby Jesus?' asked Katie.

'No,' replied Grandma, 'This is when Jesus was a grown up man. He told this story to explain something to his friends. Now, once upon a time there was a very rich man. He wanted to give a party for all his friends, to share all the good things he had with them. He sent them all invitations and they all said that they would come.'

'You mean, like Rebecca?' asked Katie.

'Just the same,' said Grandma. 'Well, on the day of the party, his servants had laid the tables with wonderful food and drinks, and he sent word to all of the guests that the party was ready. But the first guest said he couldn't come because he had just got married and he wanted to spend the time with his new wife. The second guest said that he couldn't come because he had just bought some cows that needed milking.'

'Those are silly reasons, Grandma,' said Katie. 'Didn't they want to go to the party?'

'I think they just couldn't be bothered,' said Grandma. 'Anyway, each guest in turn gave an excuse why they couldn't go to the party. They all said they were sorry to miss the party, but not one of them was able to go.

'The rich man was furious, and felt very disappointed in his friends. He told his servants to go out into the streets and invite all of the poor or sick or old people they could find to come to the party. Soon, the rich man's house was filled with people having a lovely time. Because they were poor, they enjoyed all the wonderful food all the more. They had never had such nice things to eat and drink. The rich man was glad that these people had come to his party, and said that all of his friends who refused to come didn't deserve to eat his food.'

'Well, I think his friends were all very ungrateful,' said Katie, then she went very quiet. She was thinking about Rebecca's party.

'I think it would be a shame for Rebecca to think you were ungrateful like the rich man's friends, don't you?' said Grandma gently. 'It's nice for people who offer good things to their friends to be appreciated.'

'Yes, Grandma, I think you're right. If I don't go to the party, Rebecca will think that I don't like her, and I really do. I'll wrap up the little pony for her so that I can show her that I like her.'

'I think that you will make her birthday very happy if you go and take her the pony,' said Grandma.

Just then they heard Mum calling from downstairs.

'Hurry up, Katie, or you're going to be late for the party.'

Katie's tears had dried and her hair was smooth and shiny. She and Grandma went downstairs where Mum was waiting with the present already wrapped up in new paper.

'Goodbye, Grandma,' called Katie, as she went out of the front door, 'Thank you for telling me the story.'

'Have a lovely time,' called Grandma.

Katie hurried down the path with Mum on her way to Rebecca's party.

## Poems

### Going to a party

I'm going to a party,
My hair is brushed straight,
My shoes are fresh polished;
I mustn't be late.

I've wrapped up the present
And written the card:
To write 'Happy Birthday'
Was really quite hard.

I want to start running;
The house is in sight.
The children are gathering
Under the light.

They're laughing and chatting
And jumping with glee,
'Cause through the bright window
They can just see the tea.

There's sausages, biscuits,
A beautiful cake;
There's ice cream and trifle
And jellies that shake.

The door's swinging open
And music flows out.
I can hear laughter
And singing and shouts.

It's so good to see you,
I'm so glad you came;
Thanks for the present –
Let's start the first game.

## What shall I wear?

Wear your dress with the bow at the back.
What, that old thing? It's like a sack –
That sack I used on school sports day –
I wouldn't wear it out to play.

Wear your skirt and the blouse with lace.
It gives me such a baby face!
The skirt hangs down below my knee,
No boy will ever speak to me.

Well, wear your brand new denim jeans.
You'll ask me next to eat my greens!
*No one* wears trousers any more,
And party clothes are such a bore.

I thought I'd wear my new red shorts,
The white tee shirt I wear for sports;
My friends all love the things I wear.
I'll be the best dressed person there.

What, back so soon? Is Debbie ill?
They're wearing clothes with lace and frills,
I saw them through the hall window.
I don't think now I want to go.

## Reading

### *Luke 14:12–14*

Then Jesus said to his host,
'When you give a lunch or a dinner,
do not invite your friends or your brothers,
or your relatives or your rich neighbours –
for they will invite you back,
and in this way you will be paid for what you did.

When you give a feast,
invite the poor, the crippled, the lame and the blind;
and you will be blessed,
because they are not able to pay you back.
God will repay you
on the day the good people rise from death.

## Prayers

Dear Father in heaven,
Your Son, Jesus, enjoyed parties:
We thank you for good party fun,
We thank you for good friends,
We thank you for presents
Given and received with love.
Amen

Help us, dear Father,
To give gladly to those
Who can only return
Love and thanks.
Amen.

## End of the Assembly

## Follow-up classwork

Design an invitation to a party. Design the clothes you would like to wear. Dress a cardboard doll in the clothes you have designed. Look at clothes through the ages and clothes that are worn on special occasions.

Using papier mâché, foam, tissue and junk material, make a dish of food for a special occasion:
breakfast, lunch, dinner, tea, Christmas dinner, a barbecue, a birthday party, an ice-cream dish, food from another country. Serve your meal on a suitably decorated plate.

Experiment with taste. The four taste sensations of sweet, sour, salt and bitter, are all detected in different areas of the tongue. Sweet and salt at the tip of the tongue, sourness at the sides and bitterness at the back. Work in pairs. Close your eyes when tasting. Taste with your nostrils closed. Does this make a difference?

## Further reading

**Our Street Party** M. Maris (Picture Knight)
**Brambly Hedge Winter Story** J. Barklem (Collins)
**The Surprise Party** P. Hutchins (Bodley Head)
**The Birthday Party** H. Oxenbury (Walker Books)

ASSEMBLY 2

# The picnic

## (The feeding of the five thousand)

*Matthew 14:15–21, Mark 6:35–44, Luke 9:10–17 and John 6:5–14*

---

'God will provide' is the main theme for this Assembly, which introduces the story of Jesus feeding the five thousand.

## Hymns and songs

**Five Currant Buns** (*P10*) Ten Galloping Horses (*Warne*)
**Jesus Told Wondrous Stories** (*29*) Come and Sing Some More (*Scripture Union*)
**When Jesus Lived In Galilee** (*33*) Come and Sing Some More
**Water Wagtail** (*26*) Flying a Round (*Black*)
**Row the Boat** (*27*) Flying a Round
**On The River Flows** (*28*) Flying a Round
**Michael Row the Boat Ashore** (*p75*) Knock at the Door (*Ward Lock*)

## Read the story

## The picnic

One day, Grandma and Grandpa decided to take Katie out for a picnic.

'It's going to be a special picnic,' said Grandpa, 'because we're going by boat.'

Katie was very excited. She'd never been on a boat before. As they walked down the lane to the riverbank, Grandpa picked Katie up and let her ride on his shoulders while Grandma carried the picnic basket. It was a beautiful day. The sun shone in a bright sky and from her seat high up on Grandpa's shoulders, Katie could see marsh marigolds and cuckoo flowers in the water meadows by the lane. A lark swooped and sang high above her.

'I'm hungry,' she said.

'It won't be very long before we have our picnic,' said Grandma, 'I'm sure you can wait for a little while.'

When they reached the river, Grandpa lifted Katie off his shoulders.

'Hold on to my hand,' he said. 'Your mum would be cross if you fell into the water in your dress.'

On the river bank was a notice which said, 'River ferry, every hour from 8 a.m. until sunset.' Wooden steps led down to a jetty where a large rowing boat was tied. The ferryman was sitting in the boat, waiting for people to cross the river. He smiled.

'Going across?' he asked.

Katie nodded shyly and the ferryman helped them all into his boat. The oars creaked as he rowed them across the river. Katie gazed down into the deep clear water. She thought she saw a fish dart into some weeds, but it was gone too quickly for her to be sure.

On the other side of the river there were more steps leading up from another jetty. Grandpa got out first and helped Grandma. As the ferryman lifted Katie up she realised that they'd left the picnic basket in the boat.

'They've forgotten our picnic,' she thought, and grabbed the big wicker basket. But it was too heavy for her to hold on to, and as the ferryman swung her over to Grandpa on the jetty, it slipped from her hand and fell into the water with a splash.

'I was only trying to help,' wailed Katie as Grandma helped her up the steps. Grandpa and the ferryman were fishing about in the river with a boat hook and one of the oars, but they couldn't find the basket. The movement was stirring up the mud at the bottom and by now it was hard to see anything in the murky water.

'Never mind,' said Grandpa, 'We won't find it now but I'm sure we won't starve. I'll have another look when the mud settles.'

'But I'm starving now!' cried Katie, and burst into louder tears.

'Come on,' said Grandma, 'Let's get on with enjoying ourselves.'

They led Katie into a field full of small hills, with scrubby bushes growing everywhere.

'This place is called the Humpty Dumps,' said Grandma. 'I used to play here when I was a little girl, and so did your mummy and Auntie Susan.'

'Really?' asked Katie, suddenly interested.

'Oh, yes,' said Grandma, 'They used to run up and down the little hills and build dens in the bushes. It hasn't changed much in all these years.'

'Did you play here, too, Grandpa?' asked Katie.

'No,' laughed Grandpa, 'I didn't live round here, but I used to play in places like this. I didn't even know Grandma when I was young.'

That rather surprised Katie who'd thought that Grandma and Grandpa had grown up together. Grandpa showed Katie a slow worm lying on a stone, its shiny body gleaming in the sun.

'That's a beautiful snake,' she said. Grandpa explained that it was really a lizard without legs and not a snake at all. Katie looked at him with a smile, not sure whether to believe him or not.

They watched a thrush crack a snail shell, played hide and seek, and made little pots from the muddy clay of the stream, and Katie forgot how hungry she was. She only remembered later on when Grandpa, who'd been standing on the riverbank watching some boats, called out,

'Dinner time!'

'Did you find the picnic basket, Grandpa?' she shouted, running up.

'No,' said Grandpa, spreading his big clean handkerchief on the grass, 'This is Grandpa's emergency rations.'

From various pockets, Grandpa took out a packet of nuts, a box of raisins, a packet of chocolate buttons and a bag of cheesy biscuits. He shared it all out between the three of them.

'We thank the Lord for our food today,' said Grandpa.

'We say "Thank you for the food we eat, thank you for the world so sweet," at school,' said Katie.

'That's just as good,' said Grandpa.

They all ate the food very slowly to make it last longer. Katie pretended that the cheesy biscuits were plates, and carefully balanced raisins, nuts and chocolate buttons on them.

'Cheesy biscuits taste funny with chocolate,' she said.

When all the food was gone, they sat in the shade under a tree and looked at the river.

'That dinner reminds me of a story,' said Grandma.

Katie lay on her back, looking up at the few white clouds floating slowly through the blue sky.

'One day,' said Grandma, 'Jesus was in a city, telling wonderful stories to his friends. The stories were so special that people came from all over the city to listen to him. They came from other towns and cities as well, and from the countryside around. Soon, there was not enough room for anyone else to come and listen to Jesus.

' "Follow me," said Jesus, and led all of the people out of the city and into the countryside. Now there was enough room for everyone to hear him. He stood on a rock, and all of the people sat round listening. Jesus spoke for many hours, and the crowd grew. The people were so interested in what Jesus had to say that they forgot to go home for their dinner.

'One of Jesus' friends came up to him and said, "Master, everyone is very hungry." So Jesus asked if anyone had any food, and a little boy came up to him with the lunch his mother had given him. It was two small fishes and five little loaves.

' "You can have this," said the little boy. "But it's not very much."

' "Thank you," said Jesus.

' "That's not enough for all of those people," said one of Jesus' friends.

'But Jesus took the loaves and the little fishes, and broke them up into some baskets. He filled the baskets, and kept on breaking up the bread and the fish. He filled enough baskets to feed all of the people, and by then there were more than five thousand people listening to him. Everybody had enough to eat, and nobody went home that night feeling hungry.'

'That's wonderful,' said Katie. 'It's a bit like Grandpa feeding us all from his emergency rations.'

Just then there was a shout from the river. The ferryman had come back with a longer boathook, and now that the river mud had settled again, he'd been able to spot the picnic basket lying at the bottom and hook it out. It was soaking wet, and all of the food inside was ruined, but Grandma and Grandpa were very pleased to have the basket back.

'That's very kind of you,' said Grandpa to the ferryman. 'Could we come back across now, though; I think we could all do with a cup of tea.'

'Certainly,' said the ferryman, helping Katie back into the boat, 'I expect you're pretty hungry by now, aren't you?'

'Not any more,' said Katie, telling him about Grandpa's emergency rations.

'So you won't want this apple, then?' asked the ferryman with a grin, taking out a shiny green apple from his pocket.

'Oh, yes, please,' said Katie.

## Poems

### Picnic tea

What shall we have for our picnic tea?

One chunk of cheese for a cheerful mouse,
Two green grapes for a grey woodlouse,
Three salty crisps for a silvery gnat,
Four lettuce leaves for a leather-winged bat,
Five black berries for a broad-backed bug,
Six salmon slivers for a satin-sleek slug,
Seven drops of juice for a dabbling drake,
Eight cake crumbs for a coiling snake,
Nine bent bananas for a bumble bee,
And ten tastes of everything else for me.

### The riverside

In summer time, my great desire,
When skies are clear and sun's on fire,
Is to be free and out of doors,
Beside a river bank once more.

Where damsel flies and marigolds
Share banks of reeds and grassy folds
With velvet shrews and water voles,
Who live in dark and musty holes.

Beneath the bushes, moorhens creep;
It's there the river, still and deep,
Reflects the ancient water mill
And gorse upon the distant hill.

The lock, with silent lifting gear,
Stands deep beside the restless weir.
Over the rocks the water roars;
Above, the watchful heron soars.

Yet, trapped within these airless walls,
I close my eyes and hear the calls

Of crested lapwing, heaven-bound lark,
That sing for joy from dawn till dark

And smell once more the water-mint,
Meadow-sweet, iris, cuckoo-pint,
And touch the river, cold and deep,
In dreams that haunt my waking sleep.

## Readings

### *Matthew 6:25, 26*

'This is why I tell you not to be worried about the food or drink you need in order to stay alive, or about clothes for your body.
After all, isn't life worth more than food?
And isn't the body worth more than clothes?
Look at the birds:
They do not sow seeds, gather a harvest and put it in barns;
Yet your Father in heaven takes care of them!
Aren't you worth much more than birds?'

Golden sun in a cloudless sky,
The sweet warm breath of the South wind's sigh,
Waterlilies, marigolds, trailing willow trees,
Can God have made anything more perfect than these?

## Prayer

Dear Father,
We thank you for our food.
We thank you for the many nice things there are to eat.
Let us never forget all of the children who go hungry.
We pray that you, dear Father,
Will make us generous enough to help them,
And give them the help they need to feed themselves.
Amen.

## End of the Assembly

## Follow-up classwork

Make a study of rivers. Make a model of a river with a lock, a weir, a ferry boat and pleasure craft. Make models of some of the creatures that live by the river. Paint a background of riverside trees and flowers. Have a teddy bears' picnic; make tiny plates of food for each teddy. Make sure each teddy gets the same amount of food.

## Further reading

**Grandmother Lucy Goes For a Picnic** J. Wood (Collins)
**Having a Picnic** S. Garland (Bodley Head)
**Wilberforce Goes on a Picnic** M. Gordon (Kestrel)
**Alfie and the Ferry Boat** C. Keeping (Oxford University Press)
**Jesus Feeds The People** Little Fish Books (Scripture Union)
**Thank you, God, for our day in the country** E. Reeves (Scripture Union)

ASSEMBLY 3

# Michael in the lions' den

## (Daniel in the lions' den)

*Daniel 6: 1–28*

---

This Assembly deals with the story of Daniel in the lions' den. It shows us an example of a very great faith in God, and a willingness to put complete trust in him.

The responsibilities of owning a pet could also be discussed, as well as being gentle with animals and people smaller than ourselves.

## Hymns and songs

**Old Henry the Lion** (*p40*) The Multi-Coloured Music Bus. (*Collins*)
**A Famous Lion Tamer** (*p70*) The Multi-Coloured Music Bus.
**Daniel was a man of prayer** (*36*) Junior Praise (*Marshall Pickering*)
**Have you seen the pussy cat?** (*72*) Junior Praise

## Read the story

## Michael in the lions' den

Katie was playing in the back garden in the sunshine. Mum had got out the paddling pool and the sand tray, and Katie was busily making sand pies and castles. She was also making quite a mess. When she got too hot in the sand she jumped into the paddling pool to cool off. Then, when she was cool enough, she jumped back into the sand, scattering bright drops of water everywhere. Soon it became hard to see which was the sand and which was the water.

'It's a bit of a mess,' said Mum, when she came out into the garden. 'I think it would be a good idea if you played with something else for a while so that I can tidy up. Try and find something a bit more peaceful to do.'

Grandma came out into the garden carrying a cup of tea. She laughed when she saw the mess, and put her tea down to help Katie clean herself up. She filled up a big watering can and held it high over Katie's head to wash off the sand. Katie thought that was a great game, and danced about under the spray making thunder-and-lightning noises. When the can was empty, Grandma dried her down with a big towel and helped her into a clean swimsuit.

'It's far too hot for clothes today,' she said. 'Look, why don't you play for a while in your Wendy House? It's been standing in the shade by the hedge all morning, so it should be nice and cool by now.'

'That's a good idea, Grandma,' said Katie. 'I'll just go upstairs to get some toys to play with in there.'

Katie trotted off upstairs, and was soon filling her Wendy House with an assortment of toy animals. There were horses and bears, lions and tigers, snakes and dinosaurs. Mum and Grandma soon forgot about Katie as they chatted and drank tea in the sunny garden. They didn't notice at all when she came downstairs very quietly, carrying her special picnic box closed up tightly. She went inside the Wendy House and lowered the plastic door.

After a while, Mum realised that Katie had been very good and quiet for some time.

'What are you up to in there, Katie?' she called.

Katie immediately popped her head out of the plastic door.

'Nothing. I'm just being peaceful,' she said, and popped back in.

'Too peaceful, if you ask me,' said Mum to Grandma. 'I think we'd better have a look.'

Mum and Grandma crept up to the Wendy House and looked in through the little window. Katie didn't see them. She was too busy. Her toys were all arranged in a tight circle facing inwards, and inside the circle, caught like a rat in a trap, was Michael the hamster, desperately trying to escape. He wasn't getting very far though, because every time he managed to haul his fat little body up onto a toy lion or a fluffy elephant, Katie would pick him up and put him back in the middle again.

'Katie,' said Mum sharply, 'What on earth are you doing to that hamster?'

At the sound of her mum's voice, Katie jumped. She burst into tears.

'I was only playing,' she sobbed.

Mum picked up Michael the hamster and stroked him gently.

'Poor little thing,' she said, 'You know that Michael needs to sleep in the daytime, Katie. He's a nocturnal animal. You can't treat him as though he was a stuffed toy; he's a living creature who needs to be taken care of.'

Katie just cried louder, so Mum took the exhausted hamster back to his cage. Grandma found a paper tissue to wipe Katie's eyes and nose. The little girl's face was red and blotchy from crying.

'It was far too hot for you and Michael in the Wendy House with the door down,' said Grandma. 'Come and sit with me in the shade and cool down. I'll tell you a story if you like.'

'All right, Grandma,' said Katie, still sniffling loudly.

'A long time ago, long before Jesus was born, there was a man called Daniel,' began Grandma.

'Is it Daniel Soper from my class at school?' asked Katie with a grin.

'Certainly not,' smiled Grandma, pleased that Katie had stopped crying. Just then, Mum came out with a drink of cold orange juice for Katie.

'You just drink your juice and listen to my story,' said Grandma. 'Now, Daniel was a good man. He believed in God, and prayed to him three times every day. The king, who was called Darius, was his friend. King Darius thought that Daniel was such a good man that he made him one of his special helpers, and trusted him more than anyone else. This made all of the other important people in the land jealous. They thought that Daniel was becoming too powerful and they decided to try to get rid of him.

'Some of these men went to King Darius and said that because he was such a great king, the people should worship him like a god. Anybody who worshipped any other god should be thrown into a den of lions.'

At the mention of the den of lions, Katie wriggled about on Grandma's knee with excitement.

'Well, the king was pleased,' went on Grandma, 'so he agreed to pass a new law which said that anyone who worshipped any other god but the king was to be thrown into a lions' den.

'The people who didn't like Daniel sent spies to watch him, and sure enough they soon caught him praying to God. They rushed off to King Darius and asked if the new law had been passed or not. King Darius said, "Yes, it has, and according to our ways it cannot be changed now."

' "Well, in that case you must throw Daniel to the lions", said the advisers. "We've caught him praying to his God." The king realised then that he had been tricked into passing the new law, and he was very sad. But now that the law had been made, it had to be obeyed.

'He sent for Daniel, and told his friend what had to be done. "May the God you serve save you," he said. So poor Daniel was thrown into the lions' den, and shut in there for the night. King Darius worried about Daniel all night, and as soon as the next day came, he hurried to the lions' den and opened it.

' "Daniel," called the king, "are you still alive? Has your God saved you?" Daniel came up to the king. He was unhurt. "Yes, my king," he said, "God sent his angels to stop the lions hurting me." Daniel was helped out of the den, and he and the king were happy to be together again. But the king was angry with the ministers who had tricked him and tried to make him kill Daniel. He ordered that they and all their families should be thrown into the den. And what do you think happened to them?'

Katie gazed up at Grandma with eyes big with excitement. She took the straw out of her mouth and said, 'I don't know, Grandma, what happened?'

'Well, the lions ate them all up!' said Grandma.

'Ooh, that's horrible!' said Katie.

'Yes, it is, isn't it?' said Grandma. 'Anyway, King Darius decided to make a new law, to tell the people that Daniel's God was the true God, and that they should all worship him from then on. The king knew that only the true God would have been able to save Daniel from the wild animals.'

Katie put the straw back into her mouth and made sucking noises for a while. Then she took it out and said,

'Grandma, my toys wouldn't have hurt Michael, you know. It was only a game.'

'I know that, darling,' said Grandma, 'but I expect he was very frightened.'

'Perhaps we should change Michael's name to Daniel,' said Katie, 'because he escaped from the toy lions.'

'Well, I think that might confuse everybody,' said Grandma.

'Yes, I think it would,' said Katie, 'Anyway, there's Daniel at school that I told you about. He's very naughty in class. Perhaps he should be thrown to the lions.'

Just then Mum came out into the garden with a cup of iced coffee for Grandma, and overheard Katie's last remark.

'Oh, Katie, what are you up to now?' she said.

'Only joking, Mum,' said Katie with a grin.

## Poems

### Katie's hamster

My hamster's name is Michael,
He doesn't like the light;
He sleeps all day and doesn't move
And then he plays all night.

I wake up from my sleeping
To hear a whirring sound;
It's Michael on his treadwheel
As he spins it round and round.

I see his bright eyes gleaming
As he swings from bar to bar.
If he was in the circus
He'd be a high wire star.

He nibbles seeds and carrots,
And apples green and red.
He packs them in his pouches
For a midnight feast in bed.

I want to stay and watch him
But I'm just too tired to see.
I wish he weren't nocturnal,
But diurnal, just like me.

### The lion tamer

He stands alone inside the cage,
A man alone on a floodlit stage.
He flicks his plaited bullhide whip,
A frozen smile upon his lips.
In his mind he carefully gauges
Familiar sounds from the animal cages

Of well-oiled sliding tunnel doors
And softly padding feline paws.

From the audience comes polite applause.

His face is like a sculptured mask,
As he concentrates on his daily task.
He's proud, aloof and in command,
As he makes his lonely one man stand.
The band is silent, the audience still,
As the golden beasts bound to the kill.
But he controls the cats with guile,
As he faces them with a ruthless smile.

The audience holds its breath for a while.

The lion tamer weaves and backs;
Controls the beasts with a voice that cracks
Commands, like his vicious bullhide whip.
The animals snarl and lick their lips.
They roar with a practised leonine rage
As they jostle each other and rattle the cage.
They claw the air and jump and rear
For the well-loved master they all fear.

The lion tamer bows as the audience cheer.

## Readings

### *Psalm 91: 9–13*

You have made the Lord your defender,
the Most High your protector,
and so no disaster will strike you,
no violence will come near your home.
God will put his angels in charge of you
to protect you wherever you go.
They will hold you up with their hands
to keep you from hurting your feet
on the stones.
You will trample down lions and snakes,
fierce lions and poisonous snakes.

## Prayer

### *Adapted from Psalm 104*

O Lord my God, you are very great,
You give drink to every beast of the field,
Grass for the cattle,
A refuge for the goats and rabbits,
And homes for the birds.
The earth is full of your riches.
We bless your name.

For all the creatures that live in the wild,
For all the creatures that work for us,
For all the creatures that share our homes,
We thank you Lord.
May we always care for them as you care for us.
We are all your creatures.

## End of the Assembly

## Follow-up classwork

Make a collection of books and leaflets about animal care. Make a collection of the tools needed for animal care (brushes etc.). Make a picture of your pet and say how you care for it. If you have no pet, collect and observe a snail, woodlouse or worm. Be aware of its needs, and set it free at the end of the day.

Ask a member of the R.S.P.C.A. about their work.

Visit a farm.

## Further Reading

**Happy Lion Books** L. Fatio (Bodley Head)
**Acrobat Hamster** M. Cockett (Hamish Hamilton)
**Daniel in the Lions' Den** B. Hollyer (Macdonald)

**ASSEMBLY 4**

# Party games

## (Jacob and Esau)
*Genesis 27: 1–46*

---

The story of Jacob and Esau is one of jealousy between brothers, resulting in cheating and unfairness. These themes can be discussed by the children in follow-up work, as can the differences between people, ie various facets of their appearance.

## Hymns and songs

**Heads, Shoulders, Knees and Toes** (*1*) Okki-Tokki-Unga (*Black*)
**If You're Happy** (*1*) Apusskidu (*Black*)
**Thank You For My Friends** (*31*) Tinder Box (*Black*)
**God is Pleased When We Are Friends** (*32*)
Come and Sing Some More (*Scripture Union*)

## Read the story

## Party games

Katie's birthday party was beginning to get very noisy. All of the children were getting more and more excited as they played party games, and the front room was littered with bits of paper from Pass the Parcel. After they had played Musical Chairs, they were all beginning to get tired and cross. Rebecca and Emma had started to squabble in a corner, so Grandma decided it was time for some quieter games.

'How about Squeak Piggy Squeak?' she asked the children.

'Oh, Grandma,' said Katie, 'you mean Miaow Pussy Miaow, don't you?'

'It's the same thing,' said Grandma. 'It's got different names everywhere, but I've always called it Squeak Piggy Squeak.'

'Bags I be the Piggy,' said Rebecca.

'You are a piggy,' muttered Emma, but luckily Rebecca didn't hear.

All of the children sat round quietly as Grandma explained the game to them. Rebecca was chosen to be the first to go, and she had the blindfold tied around her eyes. She carefully made her way round the children until she stopped next to one of them. Then she put the cushion on the person's lap – it was David's – and sat on the cushion.

'Squeak Piggy Squeak,' she said.

'Miaow,' said David, very softly. He grinned at the other children.

'That's not fair!' said Rebecca, 'It's supposed to be a squeak.'

'It doesn't really matter,' said Grandma, 'Any noise will do.'

Rebecca listened very carefully, but she didn't know who it was.

'Squeak Piggy Squeak,' she said again.

David had to put his hand over his mouth to stifle his giggles.

'Miaow,' he said again, just as softly as before.

'I still don't know who it is,' complained Rebecca.

'Feel his head,' called out Daniel.

'No calling out,' said Grandma, 'But it's a good idea, Rebecca. Try it.'

Rebecca ran her hand gently over David's tight curls and smiled.

'I know,' she said, 'It's David!'

When David took his turn, he sat on Harriet's lap. He couldn't tell who it was until he felt her long plaits. Harriet sat on Grandma's lap, and she knew straight away who it was because Grandma was so much bigger than the children, even though she was sitting on a low stool.

On Grandma's turn, she sat on Katie's lap, very gently.

'Squeak or Miaow, Piggy or Pussy,' said Grandma, and all the children laughed.

'Miaow,' said Katie.

'Oh, that's easy,' said Grandma, 'It's Cosmo the cat!'

They all laughed again. Grandma put out her hand and touched Katie's arm.

'It's Katie,' she said.

'How did you know, Grandma?' asked Katie.

Just then, Mum came in and said, 'Time for tea. We're having a birthday picnic here on the floor for a change. Now, if Grandma would be kind enough to tell you all a story. I can put the cloth down and bring in the food.'

The children all gathered around Grandma at the far end of the room, while Mum busily got the birthday picnic ready.

'I know a story about someone with arms like Katie,' she said, 'Would you like to hear it?'

'Yes!' shouted the children.

But Katie wasn't so sure.

'What's wrong with my arms?' she asked, pulling up the sleeve of her dress and looking at one.

'There's nothing wrong with them,' smiled Grandma, 'but there is something special about them. You have fine soft hair on your arms, just like your mum.'

'Is that all right?' asked Katie doubtfully.

'Oh, yes, lots of people have hair on their arms and legs, but yours feels special because it's so fine and soft. Like stroking a baby mouse.'

Katie smiled as she ran one hand over the other arm. David, who was next to her, touched her arm as well, and smiled.

'It's rather nice,' he said. 'My dad's got hair all over his chest, but it's very rough and curly.'

'So has my daddy,' said Harriet, 'and lots on his legs.'

All of the children started talking about hair, and Grandma had to clap her hands to get their attention.

'Shall I tell you my story?' she asked.

'Yes!' shouted all the children again, and sat quietly round Grandma to listen.

'My story,' said Grandma, 'is about a man called Esau who had hairy arms, and his brother called Jacob, who had smooth skin with hardly any hair on his arms at all. It was a very long time ago that the two brothers were born. Esau was born first, so he was the oldest, and he knew that when his father died, all of the land and animals that had belonged to his father, Isaac, would be his. This was called his birthright.

'Now, Esau loved to hunt, and he often killed an animal and cooked it for his father's dinner.'

'What sort of animal?' asked Harriet.

'It was probably a wild goat or a deer,' said Grandma. 'Now, Jacob, Esau's brother, was very sad that he had no birthright. In fact, he was very jealous of Esau, because he knew that once their father was dead, Esau would have everything and he would have nothing.

'One day, when Esau came home from a long day's hunting, Jacob was cooking some soup over a fire. Esau was very hungry, and the lovely smell of the soup made him even hungrier. He came up to his brother and said, "Jacob, I'm very hungry. Give me some of that soup you've made."

'But Jacob said, "No, not unless you give me your birthright in exchange." Well, Esau was really hungry, so he said, "All right, then. After all, if I die of hunger, my birthright won't be any use to me. Give me the soup." '

'He didn't say please,' said Daniel.

'I expect if he'd said please, then Jacob would've given him two bowls of soup,' said Katie.

'Well, as it was, he only got one bowl of soup in exchange for his birthright,' said Grandma. 'Anyway, the years went by and Isaac, the boys' father, grew old and blind. He called Esau to him and asked him to go out and catch him an animal and cook it for his dinner. He said that when Esau came back, he would give him his blessing. But his wife, Rebecca, the boys' mother, had heard what he had said to Esau, and she called Jacob to her.'

'That's the same name as me,' said Rebecca, delighted.

'It's a very pretty name, as well,' said Grandma. 'Now, Rebecca loved her son Jacob more than she loved Esau, and she wanted Jacob to have the blessing from his father instead of Esau. So she killed two small goats from their flock, then she skinned them and cooked the meat into a delicious stew. She made Jacob dress in some of his brother's clothes, and wrapped the skins of the goats around his arms, neck and chest. Jacob took the stew to his father.

' "Who's that?" asked Isaac, as Jacob entered.

"It's your son, Esau," said Jacob, "I've brought you your dinner."

"Come closer to me, my son," said the blind old man. "Let me feel your arms and neck, so that I know it's really you." So Jacob went up to his father, and Isaac felt the goat skins that Rebecca had wrapped around him. "Well, you sound like Jacob, but I can tell that you're really Esau, because you feel and smell like Esau."

' "Give me your blessing, Father," said Jacob, and his father blessed him. So Jacob had got the blessing and the birthright that should have belonged to Esau.

'A little while later,' went on Grandma, 'Esau came in to see Isaac with the stew that he had made him. "Here's the stew that you asked for, Father," he said.

'Isaac realised straight away that he'd been tricked. He said to Esau, "I'm sorry, my son, but the blessing and the birthright that should have been yours have both been given to Jacob. There's nothing I can do about it now."

'Esau was furious that he had been tricked out of everything, and he swore that he would kill Jacob. Jacob was so frightened of Esau that he had to run away to another country to escape from his brother, and he couldn't return home for many years.'

Grandma sat back in her chair and smiled at her spellbound audience.

'I liked that story because it was about me,' said Rebecca.

'It wasn't about you, silly,' said Emma.

'Well, it was the same name,' said Rebecca.

'If it was about you, then it was about me, too,' said Katie.

'There wasn't a Katie in it,' said David.

'I know,' said Katie, 'But there was someone with hairy arms like mine.' She proudly stroked the fine down on her forearms.

'Tea's ready,' called Mum.

The children had enjoyed the story so much that they had forgotten about the birthday picnic tea, and now they all remembered how hungry they were.

'But not quite as hungry as a hunter,' said Grandma with a smile.

## Poems

## Harold Hardrada

My dad, not as hairy as Harold Hardrada,*
Has a beard like a Don in the Spanish Armada.
Ginger and grey curly hair on his chest
Is hiding beneath his warm wool thermal vest.
A bandit's moustache hangs from under his nose
And forests of bristles sprout on his big toes.
Gorillas would envy his legs and his arms;
One twitch of his eyebrows would signal alarms.

But his scalp is as smooth as a hard Viking helmet,
With a fringe of fine hair like a plush curtain pelmet.
He pours tonics and lotions all over his head

*Harold Hardrada was a Viking warrior whose army was defeated by Harold Godwinson before the Battle of Hastings.

And scrubs and massages until he is red,
But try as he might, (and he couldn't try harder)
He's still not as hairy as Harold Hardrada.

## Party games

We played Blind Man's Buff,
And then Musical Chairs.
When Derek was sick
Someone took him upstairs.

We Hunted the Thimble
And played Truth or Dare,
Then Mark got a nosebleed
In Father's armchair.

We danced to the music,
We wriggled and jumped;
It ended when Lawrence
And David got thumped.

While Passing the Parcel,
Craig grabbed the last prize,
And splashed green soap bubbles
Right into his eyes.

Barry was cheating,
And argued with Ruth.
He fell on a table,
And loosened a tooth.

Jamie got angry
And started to sulk,
When Georgina called him
'Incredible Hulk'.

He went to his bedroom
And shouted some names.
We didn't much miss him;
We still played the games.

Jamie's small brother,
Who's only just four,

Dropped chocolate chip ice cream
All over the floor.

No one had noticed
Till he'd gone to bed,
Then David slipped on it
And bumped his poor head.

Thanks for the party,
The games were the best;
We think you'll feel better
When you've had a rest.

## Reading

### *Genesis 27: 28–29*

Isaac's Blessing

'May God give you dew from heaven and make your fields fertile!
May he give you plenty of corn and wine!
May nations be your servants, and may peoples bow down before you.
May you rule over all your relatives, and may your mother's descendants bow down before you.
May those who curse you be cursed, and may those who bless you be blessed.'

## Prayers

Dear God,
Some people are unkind, and some people cheat.
It's difficult to be good and kind all the time,
But please help us to try to be.
Amen.

Dear Father in Heaven,
You made all of your children different.
Some of us are short, some are tall,
Some are fat and some are thin.
Some of us are healthy, and some are often ill,
Some have to spend most of their time in wheelchairs.

Some of us have sick or injured minds.
But whatever we are, help us to remember that we are your children,
And that you made us and love us all.
Amen.

## End of the Assembly

## Follow-up classwork

Look at Brueghel's painting of children's games. Make a composite picture of present day children's games.

Make Venn diagrams of present day games; those with a ball, skipping, running, cards etc.

Invent your own board game or card game and introduce it to your friends.

Look at games through the ages.

Explore sense of touch using a collection of rough, smooth, soft, hard things etc in a 'feelie' bag.

## Further reading

**Kate's Party** J. Solomon (Hamilton)
**My Naughty Little Sister at The Party** D. Edwards (Faber)
See also reading for The party (Assembly 1)

ASSEMBLY 5

# Christmas

## (What you do for others, you do for Jesus)
*Matthew 25: 31–46*

---

The main theme of this Christmas Assembly is that what you do for other people, you do for Jesus. The gift that Katie was able to give to her friend when she stepped down from the angel's part in the school play, was a true gift for Jesus. The children can also discuss:

The celebration of Jesus' birth,
Kindness and generosity to our friends,
How to cope with disappointment,
The joy of giving.

## Hymns and songs

**Away in a Manger** (*49*) Sing to God (*Scripture Union*)
**Come in, Come in** (*47*) Come and Sing Some More (*Scripture Union*)
**Ding Dong, Ding Dong** (*48*) Come and Sing Some More
**Come They Told Me** (*11*) Carol Gaily Carol (*Black*)
**Girls and Boys Leave Your Toys** (*12*) Carol Gaily Carol
**What Shall I Give to the Child in the Manger?** (*26*) Carol Gaily Carol

## Read the story

### Christmas

'It's measles, I'm afraid,' said Dr Johns.

'Oh, no,' said Katie, 'Does that mean I can't go to school?'

'I'm afraid so,' said Dr. Johns with a smile. 'Do you mean you really want to go to school?'

'Oh, yes,' said Katie. 'This week they're going to choose the people for our Christmas play. If I'm not there I won't get a good part, and I did want to be an angel.'

'Well, I'm afraid you're just going to spend your time getting better, instead,' said Mum. 'That's the most important thing at the moment. I'm sure there will still be a part for you when you get back to school.'

So poor Katie had to spend the next few days in bed. She felt hot and spotty, and her eyes ached. Mum gave her a pair of sunglasses to wear and soothed her spots with calamine lotion. Before long, all the spots had gone, and Katie was well enough to go back to school.

As she had expected, most of the parts in the play had been taken by other children. The only part left for Katie was one of the shepherds. She watched with envy while her friends who were going to be angels made wings with beautiful crepe paper feathers. At rehearsals, they wore long white dresses and sparkling tinsel headbands that their mothers had made. As a shepherd, Katie's costume was an old striped dressing gown and a teatowel over her head. She thought it looked awful.

'You'll have some lines to say, Katie,' said Mrs Maine. 'There are three shepherds, and they say their lines together. I do hope you can learn them in time; all the other children started getting ready for the play while you were home with the measles.'

But having lines to say didn't make Katie feel any happier. The angels didn't say anything, but they looked so beautiful. The most beautiful of all was Zoe. She had long fair hair that she normally wore in two plaits. For the play, her hair had been brushed out, and it fell in shiny waves almost down to her waist. As chief angel, she had to do a little dance around the crib. That was to be the angels' gift to the baby Jesus.

But Zoe was Katie's friend, and Katie didn't want to let her know how jealous she was. So when Zoe practised her dance in the playground, Katie danced with her, until Katie knew the dance as well as Zoe did.

Two weeks before the play was performed, Zoe was taken home from school in the middle of the day because she wasn't feeling well. The next day, Zoe's mother sent Mrs Maine a note saying that Zoe had measles.

'Oh, dear,' said Mrs Maine, 'I don't think there will be time to teach anyone else to do the angel's dance. I'm afraid we shall have to leave it out of the play.'

Katie immediately put her hand up.

'Please, Mrs Maine,' she said, 'I can do Zoe's dance. Can I be an angel?'

Mrs Maine knew how much Katie had wanted to be an

angel. She smiled and said, 'Why, certainly Katie, if your mummy can make you a white dress and a tinsel headband. I'm sure you'll make a fine angel. I think we can get along with only two shepherds.'

Katie was so happy. Being an angel in the Christmas play was what she had wanted all year. She didn't think for a moment about how sad Zoe would be feeling. She finished sticking feathers to Zoe's wings, and her mum made her costume. When the class had learnt the last Christmas carol, they would be ready to put the play on. Katie was very excited when she told Grandma about the play on the telephone.

'You are coming, aren't you, Grandma?' she asked. 'Mummy's bringing Alexander, and Auntie Sue's coming with little Jenny. Peggy and Brenda are coming as well.'

Peggy and Brenda were two ladies who lived in the same street as Katie, and were her special friends.

But Grandma said that, though she would have been delighted to go to the play, she and Grandpa had already arranged to spend that week with her Aunt Hilda and Uncle Fred.

Katie was a little disappointed, but she was more surprised that Grandma should have an aunt and uncle.

'Gosh, Grandma,' she said, 'they must be ever so old.'

'Well, they're not all that old,' laughed Grandma. 'After all, I'm not *so very* old, myself, you know. But I shall be disappointed to miss your Christmas play. Your mum told me that you were going to be an angel, and that you looked very pretty in your costume.'

'I've got an idea,' said Katie. 'I could show you our school play myself, on Saturday when I come to your house.'

'How could you do that?' asked Grandma.

'Wait and see,' said Katie.

On Saturday, Katie's dad took her over to Grandma's house, so that Katie and Grandma could make their special Christmas presents for the family. He carefully carried Katie's angel costume from the car into Grandma's house and hung it on a door.

'What's that for?' asked Grandma.

'Wait and see,' said Katie.

Katie and Grandma started to make their Christmas presents. This year, they were giving people calendars. All through the year, they had pressed and dried flowers and leaves, and now they had quite a collection. Grandma got out the glue, and Katie stuck flowers and leaves on some white card, in pretty patterns. When they had done that, they stuck some small calendars beneath the flowers. They looked very pretty. Grandma put them all in the kitchen to dry.

'Now,' said Katie, 'it's time for the Christmas play. Would you like to take a seat, madam?'

Grandma sat down and Katie started the play.

'This is our Christmas play,' she said, in an important sort of voice. 'It's called a Nativity Play. I, myself, shall take all of the parts.

'This play is all about when the baby Jesus was born, in the middle of the winter, long ago. It's about all of the nice things people do for him when he's born, and the gifts they give him. The first person is an Innkeeper.'

Katie went into the kitchen and got a teatowel, which she put over her head.

'I am the Innkeeper,' she said. 'This poor woman is about to have her baby, and she has nowhere to stay. I shall give her free lodgings in my stables.'

Katie took the teatowel off, and said, 'I am a cow. I will give the mother fresh warm milk to drink. Mooo.

'I am a sheep. I will give some of my wool to keep the baby warm. Baaa baaa.

'I am a hen. I will give the mother and father fresh eggs to eat. Cluck cluck.'

Then Katie put the teatowel back on.

'I'm being three people now, all right?' she whispered, then went on, 'We are three shepherds. An angel told us about the new-born king, and we are coming to visit him. We bring soft sheepskins to wrap around the baby.'

Katie took off the teatowel.

'I'm still three people,' she said, 'but I don't know how to do a turban.'

She walked up and down a bit, with her hands folded in front of her, looking very proud and solemn.

'We are three kings from the East. We followed the star to find the new-born king. We bring gold, frankincense and myrrh.'

Then, finally, Katie slipped the long white dress over her jeans and tee shirt, and put on the tinsel headband.

'I am the chief angel, sent to guard the baby. I will dance for him.'

And Katie did the dance that she had learned from Zoe. She

did look lovely, dancing in front of the sunny window. The light reflected from her tinsel crown, and her dress floated around her in soft folds. Grandma was delighted, and when she had finished, she clapped enthusiastically. Katie bowed.

'Thank you,' she said. 'Now, to finish, we all sing a song about the baby being born, and the gifts we can give him, and then all the children who didn't want to be in the play bring presents for the baby Jesus. Everybody in the class brought a present in, and after the play is all finished, we are going to send them to the poor children who don't have many toys.'

Katie stood and sang 'In the Bleak Midwinter'. Grandma particularly liked the last verse, which said;

'What can I give him, poor as I am?

'If I were a shepherd, I would bring a lamb.

'If I were a wise man, I would do my part,

'Yet what I can, I give him,

'Give my heart.'

'That was lovely, Katie,' said Grandma. 'I shan't feel sad about missing the play, now, because you have shown it to me. Thank you.'

'There's just one thing,' said Katie. 'It doesn't seem fair, although we say that all the presents are for the baby Jesus, we give them to other children instead. That's not really giving them to Jesus, is it?'

'Oh, yes, it is,' said Grandma, 'Jesus told us, in the Bible, that every kind thing we do or gift we give to other people, if we do it in his name, we are doing it, or giving it, to him.'

'That's all right, then,' said Katie, 'I'm glad you told me that. Because it is Jesus' birthday, after all. But I'm only giving some toys that I don't really want any more. Do you think that's a good enough present for Jesus?'

'I'm sure it will be fine,' said Grandma, 'unless, of course, you'd like to give him a calendar, as well.'

They both laughed. Once the glue had dried on the calendars, Grandma threaded wool through the top to hang them up, and they were ready.

There were only a few days to go before the play was to be put on. Katie was so excited. Her white dress was hanging behind her bedroom door, and it was the last thing she looked at before she went to sleep, and the first thing she looked at when she woke up. Sometimes, she even dreamed about dancing on the stage.

But the day before the play, Zoe came back to school.

'Oh, dear,' said Mrs Maine, 'whatever are we going to do? I don't think there would be room on stage for two angels to dance; one of you might knock over the crib.'

Katie had to bite her lip to stop herself from crying. She looked at Zoe, who still had the marks from measles on her face. Poor Zoe did cry. She'd been very sick, and was only just feeling well enough to come to school. She had been looking forward so much to being in the school play, and now it looked like Katie had taken her part.

Katie thought about what Grandma had said. Anything nice that you do for someone else, or anything that you give them, if it is in Jesus' name, then it's the same as giving it to Jesus. This was the gift that she could give to Jesus for his birthday.

'It's all right, Mrs Maine,' she said, 'Zoe can be the angel. I'll be a shepherd again. After all, there should really be three, you know.'

'Of course there should,' said Mrs Maine, relieved. 'Good girl, Katie.'

'Thank you, Katie,' said Zoe. 'You're very kind.'

Mrs Maine and Zoe both knew how much Katie had wanted to be an angel, and how much she was giving up.

But Katie was happy. By giving up what she had wanted so much, she knew that she was giving a really precious gift to Jesus. It had been the thing she wanted most, and it made her think of the carol she had sung to Grandma.

'Yet what I can, I give him,
'Give my heart.'

## Poems

## The nativity play

The actors are ready,
Their costumes are neat,
The audience whisper
And shuffle their feet.

Mary's blue headscarf
Is tied at her chin,
And Joseph's brown beard
Is secured with a pin.

A shepherd is swinging
His lamb by the tail,
And one of the wise men
Is biting his nails.

The angels all giggle;
One waves to her mum.
The donkey is tired
And sucking his thumb.

'Away in a manger,
No crib for a bed.'
Malcolm is singing
And scratching his head.

Jessica's doll
Is asleep in the hay.
Everyone loves
The nativity play.

## In Bethlehem

On the cold Judean hills
Startled sheep are bleating.
From the clouded midnight sky
An angel brings God's greeting.
Wake, you shepherds, rub your eyes,
Stop your hesitating.
Through the dark night journey on;
Mary's child is waiting
In Bethlehem.

Through the bitter winter's night
Eastern kings are riding.
Behind the dark sky's scudding clouds
The wandering star is hiding.
Ride, you kings, throughout the storm,
Though the snow is flying;
In the stable you will find
Mary's child lying,
In Bethlehem.

At this happy Christmas time,
With the joy of meeting
Neighbours, friends and family,
Exchanging gifts and greetings,
Keep in your hearts that winter night
When Heaven's bells were pealing;
Before the Christ child and his kin
Kings and shepherds kneeling,
In Bethlehem.

## Is there room

'Is there room,' said the man
'For the babe to be born?'
'There's room,' said the goat,
With the broken horn.

'Is there room,' said the man
'For the donkey to rest?'
'There's room,' said the dove,
From her cosy nest.

'Is there room,' said the man
'For the angel tall?'
'There's room,' said the bat,
That hangs by the wall.

'Is there room,' said the man,
'For the shepherd band?'
'There's room,' said the beetle,
That hides in the sand.

'Is there room,' said the man,
'For the noble kings?'
'There's room,' said the moth
With folded wings.

'Is there room,' said the man,
'For children small?'
'There's room,' said the animals
That stand in the stall.

'There's room,' said the animals
'For everyone

To come to the stable
To see God's Son.'

## Reading

### *Luke 2:8–14*

There were some shepherds in that part of the country who were spending the night in the fields, taking care of their flocks.

An angel of the Lord appeared to them, and the glory of the Lord shone over them.

They were terribly afraid, but the angel said to them, 'Don't be afraid! I am here with good news for you, which will bring great joy to all the people.

This very day in David's town your Saviour was born – Christ the Lord!

And this is what will prove it to you; you will find a baby wrapped in strips of cloth and lying in a manger.

Suddenly a great army of heaven's angels appeared with the angel, singing praises to God:

'Glory to God in the highest heaven,
and peace on earth to those with whom he is pleased!'

## Prayers

What can I give him,
Poor as I am?
If I were a shepherd
I would bring a lamb;
If I were a wise man,
I would do my part;
Yet what I can I give him –
Give my heart.

*Christina Rossetti 1830–94*

What shall we give to Mary's son:
Give our courage, give our strength,
Give our friendship, give our fun,
Give our time and gentleness,
Give to all, refuse no-one.
Give to all in Jesus' name
And give your love to Mary's son.
Amen.

## Follow-up classwork

Make a Nativity scene, using plastic bottles to make the animals, angels and people. Make a rocky background for the stable using boxes and fine cloth soaked in plaster.

Look at stars and comets.

Make a graph showing how many children have had measles, chicken pox, mumps, whooping cough etc.

## Further reading

**Emma and the Measles** G. Wolde (Hodder & Stoughton)
**The Nativity Play** N. Butterworth & M. Inkpen (Hodder& Stoughton)
**Thomas and the Christmas Presents** A. Vesey (Methuen)
**Gus was a Christmas Ghost** J. Thayer (World's Work)
**The Christmas Donkey** Little Fish Books
**The Camel's Journey** (Scripture Union)
**Jesus is Born**
**The Christmas Story** – boxed set of three books
**The Shepherds and the Angels** Little Fish Christmas
**The Innkeeper and the Stable** Books
**The Wise Men and Their Journey** (Scripture Union)

ASSEMBLY 6

# Mrs Morgan's mite

## (The widow's mite)

*Luke 21: 1–4*

---

Mrs Morgan's mite introduces the children to the story of the widow's mite, and shows them that, although some people may not have much to give, they can often be more generous than those with great wealth.
Further themes which can be discussed are:
  Not showing off in front of others,
  Not judging by appearances.

## Songs and hymns

**Because You Care** (*31*) Every Colour Under the Sun (*Ward Lock.*)
**The Hungry Man** (*32*) Every Colour Under the Sun
**Working Together** (*37*) Every Colour Under the Sun
**When I needed a Neighbour** (*35*) Someone's Singing Lord (*Black*)

## Read the story

## Mrs Morgan's mite

Katie and her mum were delivering leaflets all around the nearby streets. The leaflets said that there was going to be a bring and buy sale to raise money to help the starving people in Africa. The sale was going to be held next Saturday in the Church hall, and the leaflet asked people to bring whatever they could to the hall by Friday. Katie was pleased when Mum said that she could help.

'Why can't we just send food to Africa?' she asked.

'Oh, it's much too far away, darling,' answered Mum. 'By the time the food got there, it would be spoiled. Besides, it would cost too much to post it. Do you remember, we had to pay over £1 to send Auntie Pam in Canada her Christmas present?'

'Yes, I remember,' said Katie. 'Doesn't it cost very much to send money, then?'

'No, in fact, we can give the money to the man in the bank, and he will make sure that it goes to Africa,' explained Mum.

When Friday came, Katie and her mum went to the Church hall where some of Mum's friends were already setting up the long trestle tables to hold all of the things that they were going to sell. People had been arriving all day with all sorts of things. There were boxes of tinned foods, heaps of fresh fruit and vegetables from people's gardens, home made cakes and biscuits, pots of jam, marmalade and chutney and neat piles of clothes and toys that children didn't need any more. Everybody worked hard to load all the tables with the goods and make them look especially nice. Katie helped on the baby clothes table. Mum had given her a bag of her little brother's old clothes to put on the table. As she laid out the little jackets and jumpers neatly, she heard her mum talking on the telephone at the end of the hall. She was talking to Katie's grandma.

'We're still setting up the tables,' she was saying. 'I think we could do with some more help. Can you spare a couple of hours to give us a hand?'

Half an hour later, Grandma came in to the hall. Katie ran up and gave her a kiss, and Mum asked Grandma to sort out the food table. Katie and Grandma arranged all the tins, jars and bottles on a clean paper tablecloth. Katie put all the vegetables neatly at one end while Grandma put the puddings and fruit at the other.

People carried on arriving with things to sell all afternoon. Mrs Hedges brought a box of home made cakes with pink and white icing, Mrs Mindy brought a basket of big green cabbages from her market garden and Mr Lodge brought a huge tray of sausage rolls from his butcher's shop.

'We'll sell those nice and hot at the tea table,' said Mum, 'That's just what people will want if it's a cold day like today.'

Mr and Mrs Oliver came into the hall, carrying two bird tables that Mr Oliver had made.

'We've got one like that at home,' Katie told Grandma.

'So have I,' smiled Grandma. 'I think most people in the village have got one of those!'

Eventually, all the tables were ready, and most of the helpers had gone home. Mum and the vicar were talking at the far end of the hall, and Katie was sticking price labels on the tins and jars as Grandma wrote them out. Just then, old Mrs Morgan came into the hall, took a small tin of meat and one of mixed vegetables from her handbag and put them on Katie's table. She smiled quickly round the hall and left without a word.

'Grandma, look,' said Katie, when Mrs Morgan had gone. 'Mrs Morgan only gave two little tins of food. Everybody else gave much more! That's a bit mean.'

Grandma had seen Mrs Morgan come in, and had stopped writing prices on labels to give her a smile that the old lady hadn't noticed.

'Come and sit on my lap, Katie,' said Grandma. 'I think we're both a bit tired after this long day. I'll tell you a story.'

Katie was happy to stop work and sat on Grandma's lap with her thumb in her mouth. She settled down with a little wriggle, took her thumb out and said, 'Is it a Jesus story, Grandma?'

'Yes, it's a story that Jesus told about a very rich man. He was so rich that he could buy anything he wanted. Although he had lots of rich friends, he had more money than any of them. Well, one day, this man and his friends went to the temple to pray.'

'Is that like a church?' asked Katie.

'Yes,' said Grandma. 'Now, outside the temple was a great big stone jar for people to put money in to help the poor. As the rich man came up with his friends, he told one of his servants to drop in a large bag of coins. Everybody was watching this, and they all said what a good man he was to give so much money. The rich man was very pleased. He was proud that everybody could see how generous he was, and anyway he knew he wouldn't miss the money because he had so much more at home. To him it was nothing because he was so rich. All of his friends came up behind and they all put money in the pot as well. The rich man and his friends went off into the temple, all very pleased with themselves. A little later, a widow came quietly up to the pot, and, when nobody else was looking, she put in two tiny coins called mites, and crept away again.'

'What's a mite?' asked Katie.

'It was the smallest coin they had in those days, like we have a penny nowadays,' said Grandma. 'Well, these two little coins were all the money that the widow had. She didn't have any more money at home like the rich man; she had given everything she owned. Now, when Jesus told this story, he asked his friends a question. It was this: which one had given the most, the rich man or the widow?'

Katie sat up and took her thumb out of her mouth again.

'Well, I know that the rich man gave a lot of money, but it didn't mean anything, did it? I think it was the widow,' Katie paused. 'Grandma, did Mrs Morgan give all she had?'

'I really don't know, Katie,' said Grandma, 'but I think she probably did. She's a kind old soul, and I wouldn't be surprised if that wasn't her Sunday dinner. But it was more important to her to give what she could to people who don't have anything.'

Katie felt big tears spring up in her eyes. Poor Mrs Morgan.

'Grandma, that's a very sad story. Why did Jesus make us think of sad things?'

'Jesus didn't want to make anyone feel sad, darling,' said Grandma. 'He just wanted to make us think about things a bit. Come on, let's finish sticking these labels onto the tins.'

'I haven't got any stick left,' said Katie, trying to see her tongue, 'My tongue's got all dry.'

Mum came up and said, 'How about a cup of tea?'

'What a lovely idea,' said Grandma, 'that's just what we need.'

## Poems

## The jumble sale

Lay out the socks, so carefully knotted,
Hang up the ties, all flowered or spotted.
Pile up the jumpers, some tight and some baggy,
This jacket's dogtooth check, this one is shaggy.

These sheets were made in Victorian times,
Lace-trimmed, quite yellow, embroidered with vines.
This blanket's mended and this one has shrunk,
Those are brass fire irons, don't call them junk.

Handkerchiefs, brassieres, gentlemen's pants,
Felt hats and straw hats and white elephants.
Shirts with their collars and cuffs badly frayed,
Records of operas, never been played.

A doll with an eye missing, one with no hair,
A bouncer, a dolls' pram, a grey teddy bear.
Stand by, get ready, don't open the door
Until the church clock strikes a quarter to four.

Look out, don't panic, here they all come!
They dive on the stalls like a wild rugby scrum.
'How much is this jumper?' 'I saw that blouse first!'
They're getting so angry, I think they might burst.

'It's ten pence.' 'It's fifty pence.' What was that tearing?
'Don't take that coat, it's the one I was wearing!'
Cushions and pillow slips fly through the air.
'I've only found one shoe, there should be a pair.'

The money is piled in the tins and the bags,
And all that is left is a huge pile of rags.
'Thank goodness it's over!' the helpers all wail,
'Let somebody else do the next jumble sale.'

## Tiny

A tiny helping, if you please,
Of cabbage, carrots, leeks or peas;
And give me just a little plaice,
Or I will pull a dreadful face.
I have been known to sulk and glower
When served a plate of cauliflower,
And more than half an inch of liver
Makes my cheeks and eyebrows quiver.

But serve me ice cream, with a spade
And barrels full of lemonade
Please pile my plate with golden chips
And bags of crisps with salad dips,
Fish fingers, sausage, chocolate cake,
Enough to make my back teeth ache.

I know these things are bad for me,
So when you ask me out to tea,
A tiny helping, if you please,
Of wholemeal bread and cottage cheese.

## Prayers

Dear God,
In this country, we are lucky to have so many of your good gifts:
Warm sunshine without scorching heat;
Plentiful rain without devastating floods;
Fresh winds without hurricanes or tornados.
With all these gifts, our farmers can grow all the food we need.
Please help us to remember all those people in other countries,
Who are starving because of their climate.
Make us always thankful for what we have,
And always willing to help those less fortunate.
Amen.

What can I give?
I don't have a bank account
Or lots of pocket money,
Or expensive toys.
So I'll give some time to visit the old lady next door,
Who is very lonely.
I'll wash up when Mum is busy,
I'll help to dress my little brother.
I'll say 'NO' when people want me to do wrong,
But I'll do what I'm asked to by Mum or my teacher.
I might sometimes forget,
But with God's help, I will remember.
Amen.

## Readings

### *Matthew 6: 3–4*

But when you help a needy person, do it in such a way that even your closest friend will not know about it.
Then it will be a private matter.
And your Father who sees what you do in private, will reward you.

## End of the Assembly

## Follow-up classwork

Collect and display used toys and books for a sale. Label each item with the price. Sort: soft toys, wooden toys, plastic toys and metal toys. Sort story books from information books. How else could you arrange your display? By colour, or by price? Decide on a charity for the proceeds of your sale. Write a letter to the charity, enclosing your money as a postal order or a cheque.

Find out as much as you can about different charities and the work they do.

## Further reading

**Topsy and Tim at the Jumble sale** J. & G. Adamson (Blackie)
**Dora the Storer** H. East & K. Ken (Macdonald)

**ASSEMBLY 7**

# Baby Elizabeth

## (The story of Zechariah)

*Luke 1:5–25 and 57–66*

---

This Assembly introduces the idea of accepting God's will, illustrating this with the story of Zechariah, the father of John the Baptist. It is hoped that in follow-up discussion, the following can be dealt with:

Family relationships, accepting new members into the family.

Accepting life's difficulties, and realising that we cannot always understand God's purpose.

## Hymns and songs

**Rock a Bye Baby** (*p12*) Knock at the Door (*Ward Lock*)
**Hush Little Baby** (*p30*) Ten Galloping Horses (*Warne*)
**Babies** (*p63*) Ten Galloping Horses

## Read the story

## Baby Elizabeth

All the time that Katie's mum was expecting her new baby, Katie had been telling everybody that the new baby's name was going to be Elizabeth.

'It's a lovely name,' she told people, 'and it's got a Z in it. You could call her Lizzie for short if you wanted to, but I shall always say Elizabeth.'

'Well, remember that the baby might be a boy,' said Mum.

Katie looked at her mum in astonishment.

'But it's going to be a little girl,' she said. 'She can play with me, and when she's bigger, she can wear my dresses.'

When Mum came home from the hospital with little Alexander, Katie crept in to see the tiny baby who was fast asleep, wrapped in her old shawl. She peered doubtfully at the red-faced creature.

'Say hello to your new brother,' said Mum.

'Hello, Elizabeth,' said Katie, and left the room. She thought about her new brother for a long time. She did love him, but she had wanted a little sister to play with. She decided that she wouldn't call him Alexander, but Elizabeth instead. Even though she had to admit that he was a little boy, she still wanted him to have the pretty name she had decided on before he was born.

So whenever anyone asked to see the new baby, Katie always stepped forward and said, 'Yes, I'll take you to see him. His name's Elizabeth.'

After a few weeks, Mum decided to ask Grandma to talk to Katie about the baby's name. That night, while Grandma was babysitting, she took Katie up to get ready for bed. Once Katie had washed her face and cleaned her teeth, Grandma tucked her up warmly in her quilt, and sat by the side of the bed.

'Would you like to hear a story?' asked Grandma.

Katie nodded, with her thumb in her mouth. She suddenly took it out and asked,

'Is it a story about not calling my baby brother Elizabeth?'

'Why don't you listen?' said Grandma with a smile. 'It's a nice story, I promise.'

'All right,' said Katie, and put her thumb back in.

'Once upon a time, just before Jesus was born, there was a man called Zechariah. He had a wife called Elizabeth.'

'Is it a story about a lady called Elizabeth?' asked Katie.

'Well, partly,' said Grandma. 'You'd find out if you'd let me tell you.'

'All right,' said Katie. Back went the thumb.

'Zechariah and Elizabeth were getting quite old, and they didn't have any children, which made them very sad. Elizabeth thought that she had grown too old to have children any more. But one day, God sent one of his angels to talk to Zechariah. The angel told Zechariah that Elizabeth was going to have a baby, and that the baby's name would be John. But Zechariah didn't believe the angel.

' "That's impossible," he said, "She's too old to have a baby."

'Well, this made the angel angry. "This is God's word," he said. "You have no right to disbelieve the word of God. To punish you, you will be struck dumb until God releases your tongue." '

'What's struck dumb, Grandma?' asked Katie.

'It means that Zechariah couldn't speak. He couldn't say a

word about what the angel had said to him, not even to his wife. He just opened his mouth but no sound came out.

'Soon, Elizabeth found out to her amazement that she was going to have a baby. She was delighted, and, although he couldn't say so, Zechariah was, too. After her baby son had been born, Elizabeth and Zechariah took him to the church to be named.'

'Like a christening?' asked Katie.

'Exactly,' said Grandma. 'When the priest asked Elizabeth what the baby was going to be called, Elizabeth said that he would be called Zechariah. It was the custom to call the first boy after his father, and everybody expected it. But Zechariah shook his head. He wrote on a piece of paper, "His name is John." Suddenly, he found that he could speak again.

'You see, God had kept his promise. He had given Zechariah a son, but he wouldn't let him speak until he had called the baby by the name that God had chosen.'

Katie smiled around her thumb.

'That's a nice story, Grandma,' she said. 'I like stories about babies. Are there any more stories about baby John?'

'Yes, there are,' replied Grandma, 'but they're for another day.'

'But, Grandma, why did God want the baby to be called John?' asked Katie. 'I think Zechariah is a better name. It's got a Z in it.'

'I don't know,' said Grandma. 'Nor did Zechariah. But he realised that he should always follow the word of God without asking questions, even when he didn't understand it. People do sometimes find that it's hard to understand God's way.'

'Do you think God wanted me to have a brother instead of a sister?' asked Katie.

'Oh, yes, I'm sure he sent you Alexander specially,' said Grandma with a smile. 'And I've got you another little surprise.'

She put a little box on Katie's bed. Katie sat up and took the lid off the box. Inside was a beautiful little baby doll in a frilly dress.

'Her name is Alexander,' said Grandma.

Katie picked up the baby doll and cuddled it. She looked up at Grandma and grinned.

'Silly Grandma,' she said. 'My brother's name is Alexander. This baby's name is Elizabeth.'

# Poems

## My little brother

My brother is the sort of boy
Who'll pull your hair and steal your toys,
And Mum says that, because he's small,
I mustn't hit him back at all.

My brother is the sort of chap
Who cuddles up on Mummy's lap,
And then he pokes his tongue at me.
I'd pinch him, but he's only three.

He makes me angry, makes me mad,
But Mum says he's not really bad,
And when he's fast asleep at night,
I must agree, she may be right.

## My baby

I saw my baby's hand today;
She waved to me from her warm bed.
She didn't make a sound at all.
'I felt it kick!' my mother said.

I saw my baby's tiny head.
The doctor measured it with care.
'Twenty weeks, it can't be more.'
But what's the colour of her hair?

I saw my baby's kicking foot,
Small as the top joint of my thumb.
'It kicks just like a footballer.'
'I don't think girls play football, Mum.'

And then the glowing screen went blank.
The doctor talked and filled a form.
Was it a girl? Perhaps a boy?
Inside my mother, safe and warm.

I saw my mother's secret smile
As she bent down to kiss my head.

'Someone to love and play with you,
Another little boy,' she said.

## Readings

### *Luke 1: 76–77*

'You my child, will be called a prophet of the Most High God. You will go ahead of the Lord to prepare his road for him, to tell his people that they will be saved by having their sins forgiven.

### *Mark 10: 13,14,16*

Some people brought children to Jesus for him to place his hands on them, but the disciples scolded the people. When Jesus noticed this, he was angry and said to the disciples, "Let the children come to me, and do not stop them, because the Kingdom of God belongs to such as these . . ."
Then he took the children in his arms, placed his hands on each of them and blessed them.

## Prayer

Dear Father,
You are the protector of children.
When your Son, Jesus, was small,
You sent him to Egypt to save him from Herod's soldiers.
Take care of us, and our brothers and sisters,
Especially the tiny ones who cannot look after themselves.
Make us always gentle and loving with them,
For your sake.
Amen.

## End of the assembly

## Follow-up classwork

Bring to school some pictures of you as a baby. Do you and your friends still look the same? How have you changed? Collect information on heights and weights of yourselves as babies, and now. Compare and make a graph of the heights and weights of your class. Make a graph of birthdays. Discuss baby care. Arrange visits by a pregnant mother, a new born baby, a baby of six months and a baby of twelve months. Make a picture chart of the things that a baby can do at each stage (including the unborn baby).

Collect Christian names from groups of people: small children, teenagers, mothers, fathers, grandparents, great grand parents. Are there names common to each group? Are names of people in the Bible still used today?

## Further reading

**The Baby's Catalogue** J. & A. Ahlberg (Kestrel)
**Has Anyone seen William?** B. Graham (Walker Books)
**Messy Baby** J. Ormerod (Walker Books)
**Ben's Baby** M. Foreman (Andersen Press)

**ASSEMBLY 8**

# Cousin Lucy's procession

## (The boy Jesus in the temple)
*Luke 3:41–52*

---

This Assembly tells the story of the boy Jesus in the temple in Jerusalem. The story explains that we owe different things to God and to our families on earth. The children can also discuss:

Obeying their parents,
Obeying the word of God,
Obedience to other forms of authority, teachers, policemen, etc.

## Songs and hymns

**God Is A Father** (*12*) Come and Sing (*Scripture Union*)
**Quickly Obey** (*44*) Come and Sing
**The Animals Went In Two By Two** (*38*) Apusskidu (*Black*)
**Everybody Loves Carnival Night** (*64*) Tinderbox (*Black*)
**The Ants Go Marching** (*p56*) Ten Galloping Horses (*Warne*)

## Read the story

## Cousin Lucy's procession

'We're just in time,' said Katie's dad. 'The procession will be starting any minute.'

'Daddy, what is a procession?' asked Katie, 'I thought we were here to see Lucy.'

'We are,' said Dad. 'Lucy's in the procession. She'll be on a trailer pulled behind a lorry, with the rest of her Sunday school class. There will be lots of trailers with people on them, and all the people will be dressed up in costumes. *That's* a procession.'

'What sort of costumes?'

'Oh, all sorts of things. You know, like fancy dress.'

'Oh, yes,' smiled Katie, 'like at Harriet's party. I was a cat. What's Lucy going to be?'

'We'll have to wait and see,' said Dad. 'Would you like to sit up on my shoulders to get a better view?'

'Yes, please,' said Katie.

She was very pleased to have the chance to sit on her daddy's shoulders. Since Alexander had been born, she didn't get the chance very often, but now he was fast asleep in his pushchair. He looked very sweet in his little stripy T-shirt and shorts. Katie liked him best when he was asleep. It gave her a chance to play with her best toys without him breaking them, and a chance to sit on her daddy's shoulders as well.

Soon, they heard the rumble of the first of the lorries as it pulled its trailer from behind Dynton House.

Every year, the procession went all through the village, and arrived at Dynton House where Lord and Lady Dynton decided which trailer was the best. Lucy had been in the procession with her Sunday school class for the last three years, and Grandma and Grandpa usually came along to help.

Katie saw Lucy's trailer come round the House, with Grandma walking along by the side. Lucy looked wonderful. She was dressed as a bumble bee. All of her Sunday school class were dressed the same way.

They wore black hoods, with hairbands on the top, and the hairbands had stars on springs bouncing around which were meant to be the bees' antennae. They also wore black leotards and tights, and stripy yellow and black jumpers. They all danced around between big cardboard flowers, and behind them was a huge yellow honeycomb made out of egg boxes.

Lucy spotted Katie, sitting up on her father's shoulders, and waved.

'Hello, Katie,' she shouted.

'I like your costume,' shouted Katie, but Lucy shook her head.

'I can't hear you,' she shouted back, 'I can't hear anything through this hood.' She carried on waving to Katie as the trailer passed on by them.

Katie thought how lovely it would be to be a bumble bee like Lucy.

Soon, all of the trailers in the procession were parked on the big gravel courtyard in front of Dynton House. It was a very exciting sight; everybody on the trailers was dressed in an interesting costume, some of them were singing and some were doing a sort of dance. Some were just sitting or standing on their trailers and waving to the crowd.

The grand front door of Dynton House opened, and Lord and Lady Dynton came out to judge the trailers. Lady Dynton was wearing a very beautiful dress, and had lots of jewellery on. Katie had seen her before in the village. She had been wearing wellington boots and a rather scruffy jacket then, and had looked quite different.

While the trailers were being judged, Dad took Katie to have a look at all of them. She particularly liked the clowns squirting water, the jugglers, and some Morris Dancers who waved their hankies and jingled their bells as they danced on the trailer.

Dad brought Katie an ice cream from a van, but she kept letting sticky drips fall onto his head, so he lifted her back down from his shoulders. When they had finished looking round, they went back to where Mum and Grandma were waiting.

Alexander's pushchair was empty, and Mum and Grandma looked very worried.

'What's happened?' asked Dad.

'Alex has disappeared!' said Mum. 'Grandma and I were looking for Grandpa, and suddenly we noticed that Alex wasn't in his pushchair any more. One minute he was asleep, the next minute he was gone.'

'Could somebody have taken him?' asked Grandma.

'Oh, no,' said Mum, 'he wouldn't let a stranger take him away. He doesn't like strangers, and you know how loudly he cries. I think he just woke up, saw something he liked the look of, and went to have a look. I'm afraid he knows how to undo the strap on his pushchair.'

Just then Grandpa appeared. He'd been parking his car.

'So he's not with you, then,' said Mum. Grandma explained to him what had happened.

'Right, then,' said Grandpa, 'Let's start looking for him straight away. Grandma and I will check the house and stables.'

'Then Katie and I will look around the trailers in case he's crept under one while it was parked,' said Dad.

'Well, I'll stay here in case he comes back on his own,' said Mum. 'But first, I think we'd better ask the man on the loudspeaker to ask people to look out for him.'

A few minutes later, the loudspeaker crackled into life, and, amongst a lot of buzzing and hissing, a voice told the crowd that a little boy called Alexander, who was dressed in a stripy T-shirt and shorts, was lost.

'What did he say?' asked Katie, 'I could hardly hear a word.'

'No,' said Dad, 'It wasn't very clear, was it? I don't think that's a very good microphone.'

They looked under every trailer, but there was no sign of Alexander. When they got back to Mum, Grandma and Grandpa were there as well. They hadn't found him either.

Mum looked very worried, and Katie thought she'd been crying. She put her hand into Mum's and said, 'Don't worry, Mum, he'll soon come back.'

'That naughty boy won't tell anyone that he's lost if he's enjoying himself,' said Dad. 'We need to see over the heads of this crowd. I think it would be best if Grandpa and I went to have a look for him now, since we're the tallest.'

'You stay here with me and your mummy, Katie,' said Grandma, 'And I'll tell you a story while we're waiting.'

'All right,' said Katie, grateful to have something to take her mind off looking for Alexander.

She and Grandma sat on the grass, on Grandma's raincoat, while Mum stayed where she'd been standing when Alexander disappeared.

'A long time ago,' began Grandma.

'When Jesus was a little boy?' interrupted Katie, then, before Grandma could answer, she said, 'I bet Jesus didn't run away from his mummy and daddy when he was little.'

'Well, as a matter of fact, he did,' said Grandma, 'And I'll tell you the story about it, if you let me.'

'All right,' said Katie.

'This is how it happened,' said Grandma. 'Now, when Jesus was a young boy, about twelve years old . . .'

'That's not little!' said Katie, 'That's older than me . . . sorry.'

Grandma looked at her, then carried on.

'As I was saying, when Jesus was a fairly young boy, his parents took him to Jerusalem for the Feast of the Passover. That was a very special time for them, when they had special food, and visited the Temple in Jerusalem to give thanks to God. It was rather like when we celebrate Jesus' birth at Christmas.

'After all the celebrations, Jesus' parents started off for home, but Jesus stayed behind in Jerusalem without telling his parents where he was. His parents, Mary and Joseph, thought that he was with other members of their family, and it was only after they had been travelling for a whole day, that they realised that he was missing.'

'Just like Alexander,' said Katie.

'Yes,' continued Grandma, 'so when they couldn't find him, they had to go all the way back to Jerusalem again, looking for him everywhere. They were worried and a bit cross. They looked for him for three days, and eventually they found him in the temple. He was sitting with the teachers, the doctors and the priests, listening to them talk and asking them questions. Everyone was amazed at how clever he was.

'Now, although Mary and Joseph were really pleased to have found him safe and well, they were also a bit angry, just like your Daddy is now.

'Mary said to Jesus, "Why have you done this to us? Your father and I have been really worried."

'But Jesus said, "Why were you looking for me? Didn't you know I'd be here, about my Father's business?" Now, Mary and Joseph didn't really understand what he meant by this, but Mary remembered this, and all the other wonderful things that had happened. She knew that her son was a very special person, and would go on to do great things.'

'But did they smack him for being naughty?' asked Katie.

'The Bible doesn't tell us that,' said Grandma, 'But it does tell us that Jesus went back to Nazareth with his parents, and did what they told him to do after that.'

'Is the story about learning to do what our parents tell us to?' asked Katie.

'Well, that was important,' said Grandma. 'You see, Jesus wouldn't have wanted to worry his parents. But for him, it was more important to learn more about his Father in Heaven.'

'I suppose it must be difficult having two fathers,' said Katie, watching her own father pushing through the crowd without Alexander.

'You have two fathers, as well,' said Grandma, 'your father on earth – Dad – and your Father in Heaven. That's God. I've heard you say "Our Father which art in Heaven" in your prayers. That means "Our Father in Heaven".'

'Yes, that's right, I do,' said Katie, 'You know, I hadn't thought about it like that.'

Dad came up to them, followed by Grandpa.

'I can't find him, or anyone who's seen him,' said Dad, 'But in this crowd, it's difficult to see anything. Even Grandpa and I can't see over everybody's heads.'

Katie had an idea.

'Perhaps if I sit on your shoulders again, I could see further,' she said.

Her dad looked a bit doubtful. His shoulders were still sore from carrying Katie for so long before, and his hair was still a bit sticky from the ice cream she had dropped on it. But he wanted to find Alexander.

'All right,' he said, 'We'll give it a try.'

As they set off, they heard the loudspeaker start to buzz and crackle again. Then it sounded as though someone had hit the microphone sharply a couple of times, and the buzzing stopped. At last, they could hear what the announcer was saying:

'The winners today are Dynton playgroup, with "The Old Woman Who Lived In a Shoe", second are "The Bumble Bees", and third are the Dynton Morris Dancers.'

With a rumble, the lorries started to move off, pulling the trailers. They passed by Katie and her dad, and all the people in fancy dress waved and cheered as they went. The Bumble Bees' trailer passed them, with Lucy and her friends all dancing and singing. They were very pleased to have come second.

'There he is!' shouted Katie.

Sure enough, there on the trailer was Alexander. He was wearing a headband with bobbing stars, and in his stripy T-shirt and shorts, he looked just like another Bumble Bee. He was waving happily with the others.

Of course, what with her hood, and the crackle on the speakers, Lucy couldn't have known that Alex was lost. She must have thought that his parents knew where he was, so she just made sure he stayed with her. He was very happy, and had had a wonderful time.

As the procession rumbled on by, Katie and her dad were both smiling with relief.

'Come on, Katie,' said Dad, 'Let's go and get Mummy, and we'll follow the Bumble Bees. When they stop, we'll collect our own little bee and take him home to tea.'

# Poems

## Cann Lane Wood

My father said
I never should
Go by myself
Through Cann Lane Wood.
If I did,
He would say,
'Naughty little girl
To disobey.
I've told you over and over again not to go to the woods alone.
Why don't you listen to me when I talk to you?
You're not listening now, are you?
Well, look at me when I'm speaking to you.
What did I say?'
'I'm very naughty to disobey,
And I won't go out to play
Today or any other day.'

My father said
I never should
Go by myself
Through Cann Lane Wood.
Because I did,
I should say
I'm a naughty little girl
To disobey.
'But, Dad, Mrs Morgan took us for a nature walk, and said get into twos.
And Debbie Moss broke friends with me, so I had to walk by myself.
On my own.
(With the rest of the class and Mrs Morgan)
In the woods.
And I found you some of your favourite mushrooms.
Now can I go out and play?

# The Genesis Procession

I'm going first, the lion said,
I need a mane and a set of claws,
Two sharp tusks and a long grey trunk,
And soft pink paws.

I'm going next, the tiger said,
Long, slim legs will suit me fine;
One green eye and a big black tusk,
And a curvy spine.

How about me, the ostrich said,
I'd like to swim in the river Nile,
So I will need some shining scales,
And a toothy smile.

I'll be next, the hedgehog said,
I'd like a coat of softest leather,
A great big pair of hopping legs,
And a purple feather.

Please don't push, the Maker said,
You'll all get served, just keep in line,
The procession looked quite orderly once –
Please read the sign.

'God reserves the sovereign right
To give you what he thinks you need.'
So keep in line or you'll get nothing;
Can't you read?

Lion, forward, here's your mane;
Tiger, you shall have some stripes;
Ostrich, two long legs for you;
Hedgehog; some spikes.

The animals joined the big parade,
Displaying all their new possessions,
God smiled, content with what he'd made,
His Genesis Procession

# Readings

## The Lord's Prayer

### *Matthew 6: 9–14*

Our Father in heaven:
May your holy name be honoured;
may your Kingdom come;
may your will be done on earth as
it is in heaven.
Give us today the food we need.
Forgive us the wrongs we have done,
as we forgive the wrongs that
others have done to us.
Do not bring us to hard testing,
but keep us safe from the Evil One.
If you forgive others the wrongs they have done to you, your Father in heaven will also forgive you. But if you do not forgive others, then your Father will not forgive the wrongs you have done.

### *Matthew 4: 14 & 16 and John 8: 12*

. . . the prophet Isaiah had said . . .
The people who live in darkness
will see a great light.
Jesus spoke . . .
'I am the light of the world' he said
'Whoever follows me will have the light
of life and will never walk in darkness.'

# Prayers

Dear Father in Heaven
There are times when I feel angry
and don't want to do as I'm told.
Sometimes I shout and stamp
and want to hit someone.
This is not your way, dear Lord.
Give us the strength to calm
our bad thoughts
and violent ways

so that we may grow
more like your son Jesus Christ.
Amen.

Day by day, dear Lord, of thee
Three things I pray;
To see thee more clearly,
Love thee more dearly,
Follow thee more nearly,
Day by day.

*Richard of Chichester (1197–1253)*

## End of the Assembly

## Follow-up classwork

Study the honey bee. Make a model of a bee. Make hexagonal prisms and put them together to make a comb. Examine the job of each kind of bee: Queen, drone, worker (nursemaid, collector, soldier, comb maker etc.). Make pupae for the comb.

Act one of the stories of the Old Testament, and take it to an audience in the same way that religious plays were acted in Medieval times. 'Process' with your band of players.

## Further reading

**Your Festival** R. Pollock (Cambs. Ed)
**Pied Piper** N. & T. Morris (Evans)
**Up Along, Down Along, Under & Over**
D. Wilmer & I. Schweitzer (Collins)

**ASSEMBLY 9**

# Cosmo's bath

## (Jesus washes the disciples' feet)
*John 13: 5–16*

---

This Assembly introduces the story of Jesus washing the feet of his disciples at the Last Supper. In the follow-up classwork, it is hoped that the following can be discussed:

Jesus' love for his disciples and for us.

The love within the family unit – a mother's love for her children, parent birds feeding their young, etc.

Caring for others. Who really needs our help? How can we care for others?

## Hymns and songs

**Praise Him, Praise Him** (10) Come and Sing (*Scripture Union*)
**God Takes Good Care of Me** (*14*) Come and Sing
**Hands to Work and Feet to Run** (*47*) Come and Sing
**Jesus' Hands Were Kind Hands** (*45*) Come and Sing
**Thank you Lord** (*6*) Come and Sing Some More (*Scripture Union*)
**Jesus' Love is Very Wonderful.** (*31*) Sing to God (*Scripture Union*)

## Read the story

## Cosmo's bath

Katie's mum was spring cleaning. She'd taken down all the curtains and removed the loose covers from the chairs and cushions. The washing machine had been going since very early that morning. The clothes-line was quite full, and Mum was just pegging out some of the smaller things on to another line she'd put up from the shed to one of the bigger trees.

Since Alexander was having his nap, Mum decided that it would be the best time to wash the ornaments, so she got out the old baby bath and put it on the back lawn. Katie helped her fill it up with hot soapy water, and then, while Mum washed the ornaments, Katie carefully put them on the grass in the spring sunshine to dry. When Katie got bored with that, Mum gave her a plastic pipe so that she could blow bubbles in the soapy water.

They had just finished putting all of the dry ornaments safely indoors when Alexander woke up. When he came downstairs and saw the bath full of water, quite cool by now, he wanted to play in it. Mum got some of his plastic toys for him to wash, but he got himself wetter than the toys, so she found him something else to do.

Meanwhile, Cosmo the cat was taking no interest in the spring cleaning at all. It was the time of year that the starlings nested in the roof, and he could hear the cries of the baby birds as they called to their parents for more food. Cosmo was quite sure that if he tried hard enough, he would be able to get up to the roof and catch the birds. He climbed up onto the glass roof of the conservatory, but he couldn't keep his footing on the slippery surface. With a frantic howl, he slithered back down to the edge, still trying to scrabble his way back up, and fell right into the rainwater barrel.

'Oh, Cosmo, you silly cat,' laughed Mum, as she lifted the soaking animal out of the barrel. She wrapped him up in an old towel and rubbed his fur dry.

'Silly Cosmo,' repeated Katie, taking the damp cat from her mum and carrying him up to the sunniest part of the garden to dry off. Alexander followed her, saying, 'Silly Cosmo, silly Cosmo.'

Cosmo started to clean himself, trying to look as though nothing had happened. Just then a mother starling came to the edge of the roof with a beak full of worms and grubs for her babies. As soon as the babies saw her, they started squawking and twittering for attention.

Cosmo immediately forgot the soaking he had just had and rushed down the garden for another attack on the birds. This time, he ran along the side of the house and disappeared into the front garden, looking for another way up to the roof.

Mum had gone indoors to iron the curtains while Alexander and Katie folded dusters, when Grandma suddenly appeared at the back door carrying Cosmo in her arms. Cosmo was drenched and covered in patches of green slime. He looked rather dazed.

'Oh, no,' groaned Mum, 'Whatever's that cat been up to this time?'

Grandma explained what had happened.

'Cosmo came hurtling out of the front gate after a bird just as I was arriving. Luckily I was just stopping the car or I'd have driven right over him. He tried to avoid the car, but I think he might have bumped himself a bit, because he bounced right into the ditch at the side of the road. Naturally, the bird got away.'

Mum put the cat on the floor and knelt down beside him. She gently felt through his wet fur for cuts or broken bones. Cosmo stood still while Mum wrapped him once again in an old towel and gently put him into his basket to rest. She closed the back door to keep him inside for a while.

'Well, he seems all right,' she said. 'Just a bit dazed from the bump. Let's have a cup of tea while he has a rest.'

They all went into the front room to give Cosmo some peace while he was recovering.

'I like spring cleaning,' said Katie, munching at a chocolate biscuit. 'It's nice to get everything all clean again.'

'I think your next job is going to be cleaning Cosmo up,' said Grandma. 'That ditch was full of slimy weed, and I think most of it stuck to him.'

'Well, we could wash him,' said Katie with a grin, 'but I don't think we'd better peg him out on the line to dry.'

Later on, Mum said, 'I'll just go and see if Cosmo's feeling better yet. If he's still dazed when Daddy gets home, I think we'd better take him to the vet.'

But Mum came straight back into the front room.

'He's gone,' she said. 'He can't be feeling too poorly, because he's gone straight up the chimney to the roof. He must've heard the noise of the birds through the fireplace.'

Mum, Grandma and Katie rushed out into the garden to look up at the chimney, while little Alexander looked up into the fireplace. There was a sudden scrabbling, followed by a cloud of fine soot that covered Alexander in a film of black. He stepped back from the fireplace just as Cosmo fell down the chimney in a great shower of soot and dust. The cat was black from head to tail, and his fur stuck out in spikes where it had still been damp when he climbed up the chimney.

'Silly Cosmo, silly Cosmo,' said Alexander again. He picked the filthy cat up in his arms and staggered out into the garden. The others were still busy trying to see if Cosmo had come out of the chimney yet, and didn't notice as Alexander carried the cat to the bath of cold soapy water. As he was about to dump Cosmo into the water, Mum noticed what he was doing.

'No, Alex, don't drop him in there!' she shouted, but it was too late.

Alexander didn't drop Cosmo into the water. Instead, he stepped right in still holding him, and sat down with a splash. Cosmo was so surprised that he just sat there in the water with the little boy, who was starting to rub his fur to clean off all the soot.

Grandma and Katie laughed at the sight. Then Mum started to laugh, and even Alexander joined in, just because everybody else was laughing.

Once Mum had cleaned Alexander and put him in some dry clothes, Grandma said, 'I'll tell you what, shall I take the children to the park while you finish cleaning?'

'Would you?' asked Mum gratefully, 'That would be such a help.'

As they set off for the park, Cosmo was lying in the sun in the back garden. He had been thoroughly cleaned and dried, and was having a rest from being naughty. He wasn't even looking at the birds – well, only a bit.

After Alexander and Katie had swung and slid and climbed and played as much as they could wish, they all sat together on a park bench, eating ice-creams.

'Do you think Mummy'll have finished the spring cleaning by now?' asked Katie.

'She'll be well on the way,' replied Grandma. 'But it's a big job.'

'Mummy always has to do lots of cleaning,' said Katie. 'It's not really fair, is it? Alexander and I don't do much cleaning. We just get things dirty most of the time. And I don't think Daddy does very much because he's at work all day.'

'Well, things do get dirty, so they have to be cleaned,' said Grandma.

'Can you clean everything with water?' asked Katie.

'Not at all,' said Grandma. 'For example, if you wanted to clean gloss paint off a brush, you'd have to use special cleaners. Water's fine for cleaning Cosmo's fur though. It's a pity that water won't stop him chasing birds.'

'Yes,' said Katie, thoughtfully. She paused, then asked, 'Grandma, why does Mummy work so hard to keep everything nice and clean? I know she doesn't like some of the work she does, like the ironing, but she still does it.'

'It's because she loves you all,' said Grandma, 'you, Alexander and Daddy. It's good to do even unpleasant things for the people you love. It's one of the most important things that Jesus taught us, to care for each other in every way we can.'

'Even by ironing?' asked Katie.

'Certainly,' said Grandma. 'Did you know that once, Jesus washed the feet of all his friends. Some of them said that he shouldn't wash their feet, because he was their Lord and Master. Jesus said that if he could wash their feet to show his love for them, then they should go out into the world to care for others even if it meant washing their feet.'

'Did they wash everybody's feet after that, then?' said Katie.

'I don't know, darling, but I do know that they did a lot of other kind things for people and I think that's what Jesus wanted.'

'It might not be very nice to wash some people's feet, might it, Grandma?' said Katie. 'Mummy says that Daddy has smelly feet after he plays golf. She must love him very much to wash his socks.'

Grandma smiled.

'I think that's true,' she said.

'Do you think that Alexander gave Cosmo a bath because he loves him, then?' asked Katie.

'I expect so,' said Grandma.

Alexander stopped licking his ice cream and looked up at Grandma.

'Silly, silly Cosmo,' he said, with a big smile.

## Poems

## Why should I wash?

Why should I wash?
I had a bath a week ago – or was it two?
It was the day that submarine was new.
I sank my brother's plastic duck.
And then my aeroplane got stuck
In that big fern. It crashed right down;
The soil made all the water brown.
I spilt some stuff called 'Manly Stubble'
Which made the water froth and bubble,
But still I had a wash.

Why should I wash?
That's not a boil beneath my hair,
My collar rubs my neck just there,
And those grey lines aren't really dirt,
It's only dye from my grey shirt.
I changed my socks when they got wet,
That smell is from my brother's pet,
And – wipe my nose on my school tie?
If someone said so, it's a lie!
All right, I'll have a wash.

## Cat

Prowling, howling,
Arching back when dogs are growling;
Tail fluffed out like feather dusters,
Eyes as bright as diamond clusters.

Spitting, hissing,
Tattered ears and eye-teeth missing;
Torn and broken unsheathed claws,
Matted fur on coat and paws.

Purring, crooning,
Sleek and glossy kitten grooming;
Rubbing round the one he loves,
Killer wearing velvet gloves.

Rolling, stretching,
Stuffed mouse catching, soft ball fetching;
Answering the spoon on tin,
Drops his latest bloodstained sin.

## Reading

### *John 13: 12–15*

After Jesus had washed their feet, he put his outer garment back on and returned to his place at the table. 'Do you understand what I have just done to you?' he asked. 'You call me Teacher and Lord, and it is right that you do so, because that is what I am. I, your Lord and Teacher, have just washed your feet. You, then, should wash one another's feet. I have set an example for you, so that you will do just what I have done for you.'

## Prayers

Teach us, good Lord, to serve you as you deserve,
To give and not to count the cost,
To fight and not to heed the wounds,
To toil and not to seek for rest,
To labour and not to ask for any reward,
Save that of knowing that we do thy will.
Amen.

*Ignatius Loyola*

Dear Father in Heaven,
We thank you for all of the people who take care of us,
The doctors and nurses,
The police, the firemen and the ambulance drivers,
Our grandmas and grandpas,
We thank you especially for giving us our mums and dads
Who love us, care for us and protect us.
Most of all, dear Father, we thank you
For your love and protection
That stays with us forever.
Amen.

## End of the Assembly

## Follow-up classwork

Dress in the uniform of someone who helps others. Say who you are and how you help others.

Draw or paint a picture of your mum. Say how she cares for you.

Find out how parent birds and cats care for their young.

Keeping your classroom clean; find out if dirty marks from pencil, ink, dried milk, paint or glue can be cleaned with a dry cloth, a wet cloth, washing-up liquid and a wet cloth or scouring powder and a wet cloth.

Make a collection of empty boxes and bottles that Mother uses for cleaning.

## Further reading

**Spotlight on Cats** J. & C. Spencer (Hamlyn)
**Book of Pets** G. Cansdale (Ladybird)
**Nesting Birds** W. Reade & E. Hosking (Blandford Press)
**Birds** P. Holden (Usborne)
**The Beast in the Bathtub** K. Stephens (Hyman)
**Time to Get Out of the Bath Shirley** J. Burningham (Cape)

**ASSEMBLY 10**

# An Easter donkey

## (The entry into Jerusalem)

*Luke 19:28–36, Mark 11:1–11, also Matthew 21:1–9 and John 12:14*

---

This Assembly tells the story of Jesus' entry into Jerusalem on a donkey. It introduces the themes of celebration, caring and sharing. It is hoped that in follow-up work, these themes can be discussed:

The family celebrating Easter together, and what Easter means to us,

Caring for God's creatures and for each other,

Sharing our belongings.

## Hymns and songs

**Praise King Jesus** (29) Come and Sing (*Scripture Union*)
**Stand up, Clap hands** (*16*) Come and Sing Some More (*Scripture Union*)
**Clip clop, clip clop,** (*41*) Come and Sing Some More
**Donkey story** (*42*) Come and Sing Some More
**Hurray for Jesus** (*50*) Come and Sing Some More
**We have a King who rides a donkey** (*51*) Someone's Singing, Lord (*Black*)
**Jesus rode a donkey into town** (*73*) Praise God Together (*Scripture Union*)

## Read the story

## An Easter donkey

Katie sat up in bed wearing her Easter bonnet, too excited to stay asleep. She had made the bonnet at school in the last week before the Easter holidays. It had yellow paper flowers around the brim and a curly green crepe-paper ribbon around the crown. Her teacher, Mrs Maine, had fixed some elastic to the hat so that it wouldn't blow off in the wind.

Nobody else was awake yet, not even little Alexander. Katie smiled to herself. Alexander was too small to know that today was a special day, but she knew. She reached over to her bedside cabinet for the shiny box shaped like a lorry that had been put there in the night. Inside the box, all neatly wrapped up in silver foil, was a chocolate egg that fell into two halves when she took the foil off. And inside *that* was a little packet of chocolate sweets.

Katie broke off a piece of the egg and took two chocolates from the packet, putting the rest of the egg back into the box for later. Then she got out of bed and tiptoed over to Michael the hamster's cage.

'Michael,' she called softly, 'I've got a treat for you.'

She poked a small piece of chocolate through the bars of the cage. Michael the hamster came sleepily out of his cosy bed and took the chocolate in his tiny pink paws. He popped it into his cheek pouch and pressed his nose through the bars for more.

'No, Michael,' said Katie, smiling fondly at her pet, 'You can't have any more, it's not good for you. Mummy says it makes you smell.'

Suddenly there was a noise like a creaking cough from outside. Katie ran to the window and looked out.

Behind the privet hedge at the bottom of the garden was a paddock, and in the paddock was a donkey with enormous ears. It had pushed its large head through the privet hedge and was looking into Katie's garden. As Katie stared at it, it opened its mouth and made a horrible noise like a diesel train going into a tunnel.

'Oh, the poor thing,' said Katie, 'It must have a sore throat. I'll give it a piece of Easter egg. That'll make it feel better.'

The donkey stopped braying to try nibbling at the privet. Katie quickly put on her dressing gown and slippers and crept down through the sleeping house. Even the noise the donkey had made hadn't woken anybody up yet.

Unlocking the back door, Katie stepped out into the damp garden. Bright yellow daffodils, primroses and forsythia still glistened with the rain that had fallen in the night. It was going to be a beautiful Easter Sunday.

The donkey spotted the flowers on Katie's Easter bonnet as she ran up the path towards it, carrying a piece of chocolate egg in her hand. It had never tasted chocolate before, but it knew that it liked flowers.

Katie held the chocolate out on her flat hand, underneath the donkey's velvety nose, but the donkey wasn't interested.

Instead, it bit into the flowers on Katie's bonnet and whisked it away over the hedge. Katie was horrified.

'Give me back my hat, you naughty donkey,' she cried, but the donkey shook her bonnet about then dropped it and stood on it, gazing at Katie with its soft brown eyes. The bonnet was crushed and broken beyond repair.

'I was going to wear that to church this morning,' said Katie sadly. 'You naughty, horrible donkey.'

The tears started to run down her cheeks and she turned to go back down the path. At the back door she saw her mum standing in her dressing gown, and with a sob she ran up to her with her arms held out. Mum picked her up and cuddled her.

'Whatever's the matter, darling?' she asked.

'It's that donkey up there,' sobbed Katie, 'It ate my hat. I hate donkeys. I was going to wear my Easter bonnet to church this morning.'

'It doesn't really matter what you wear, darling,' said her Mum. 'That's not the important thing about Easter.'

'It does matter, it does!' cried Katie. 'Today's a special day, so I wanted to look special too.'

'Well, I'll phone Grandma and see if she can help,' said Mum. 'Now, go and get dressed. It'll be time for breakfast soon.'

Katie went upstairs to her bedroom and looked miserably through the window to the paddock at the top of the garden. The donkey was still nibbling cautiously at the paper flowers on her squashed bonnet.

After breakfast was finished, Grandma and Grandpa arrived. Grandma was carrying a big plastic bag and Grandpa had a large cardboard box and some mysterious-looking sticks. Katie ran up to see what they had brought.

'Can I look in your bag, Grandma?' she asked. 'What's in that box, Grandpa?'

'Katie, don't be so rude,' said Mum.

But Grandma opened the plastic bag with a smile and pulled out a large straw hat.

'Why, I can remember that hat,' said Mum. 'I used to wear it when I was Katie's age. I didn't know you still had it.'

'But Grandma, it's not got any flowers on it,' complained Katie.

'Well, it's lucky that this is a good time of year to pick some beautiful flowers to decorate it with, isn't it?' said Grandma.

'Real flowers!' said Katie. 'What a lovely idea.'

'Come into the garden and help me pick some,' said Grandma, 'then Grandpa can get ready.'

'Get what ready?' asked Katie.

'Just wait and see,' said Grandpa.

Grandma and Katie went out into the back garden and had soon picked some sprigs of yellow forsythia, a small bunch of primroses and two great golden daffodil trumpets. The donkey watched them from the other side of the hedge, braying suddenly and making them both jump.

'I hate horrible donkeys,' said Katie, glaring at it.

'Oh, Katie, you mustn't hate any of God's creatures,' said Grandma. 'They can't help their nature. Donkeys just chew things up, it's the way they are. Jesus once needed a donkey for a very special job. Let's go inside now, and Grandpa can tell you all about Jesus' special job while I get your hat ready.'

Katie dashed into the house to see what Grandpa had been doing. There, on the dining room table, Grandpa had set up a cardboard box theatre. A big rectangle had been cut from the front and Grandpa was sitting at the side, which was open so that he could move the actors about. There was a fringe of green paper grass stuck to the front of the stage, and painted scenery at the back. Katie thought it was wonderful.

'Take a seat, Katie,' said Grandpa. 'You're going to see a play.'

'Oh, great,' said Katie, all excited. 'I saw a play at school once. It was about the Hobbit. Is that what this one's about?'

'No,' said Grandpa. 'Now get comfortable, the play's about to begin.'

Mum and Alexander came and sat beside Katie, and Grandma sat behind them, sewing the flowers onto the hat. Grandpa started to talk in a deep important voice.

'A very long time ago,' he began.

'Was it when Jesus was a baby?' interrupted Katie.

'No,' answered Grandpa in his normal voice. 'This was when Jesus was a grown-up man like your daddy.'

'Anyway, a long time ago,' he continued, in the deep voice again, 'there was a little donkey who lived in a field in a village near Jerusalem.'

From the side of the stage, Grandpa pushed forward a little brown cardboard donkey, stuck to the end of a long stick. He wiggled the stick up and down and the little donkey looked as if it was eating the paper grass at the edge of the stage.

'One day, Jesus was going to go into Jerusalem, and he asked two of his friends to go into the village to find him a donkey to ride on.'

Grandpa put little figures of Jesus and two disciples onto the stage.

'Jesus told his friends that they would find a donkey in the first field they came to. He said that they should bring the donkey to him, and that if anyone tried to stop them, they should say, "The Master needs him".

'So the two men went into the village and came to the field where the little donkey was grazing. The owner came up to them and said, "What are you doing?" and the two disciples said, "The Master needs this donkey".

' "Take him" said the owner; he was happy to let them.

'The donkey let Jesus sit on his back. He trotted proudly into Jerusalem carrying the King of Heaven on his back while the people cheered and shouted Hosannah, and threw down palm leaves for them to walk on.'

Everybody clapped and cheered as the play finished and Grandpa put away all of his sticks and figures. Katie's dad came in to the dining room to tell them that it was almost time to go to church.

'Come and see your new Easter bonnet, Katie,' said Grandma, putting down her needle and thread. The old straw hat was covered in the yellow flowers from the garden.

'Oh, Grandma,' breathed Katie, 'it's lovely!'

Grandma tied the ribbons under Katie's chin, and the whole family left for church.

Later that day, Mr Harding, who owned the paddock at the end of the garden, found the battered remains of Katie's old bonnet. He called over the hedge, 'Is this your bonnet, Katie?'

'Well, it was,' said Katie, 'But my grandma made me a lovely new one.'

'I'm sorry Pixie got at this one,' said Mr Harding. 'How would you like to have a ride on her back to make up for it?'

'Can I really?' asked Katie.

'Oh, yes, Pixie loves to give children rides. She used to work every summer giving rides at the seaside. She's very gentle, but I'm afraid that she does love to eat flowers.'

Katie took off her new bonnet and laid it carefully on the ground well out of Pixie's reach. Mr Harding helped her over the hedge to ride around the paddock on the donkey's back.

Afterwards, she gave Pixie a small apple.

'That's because we're friends now. You can't have any Easter egg because I've eaten all mine.'

Mr Harding picked up Katie's old hat and straightened out some of the worst dents.

'Would you like it back?' he asked.

Katie just shook her head.

Mr Harding put the battered bonnet between the donkey's ears and fixed the elastic to her halter to keep it on.

'There, now Pixie has an Easter bonnet, as well!'

Katie laughed, and Pixie shook her head and brayed as though she wanted to join in with the laughter.

## Poems

### Easter

Frost still ices ponds and ditches
On high moors and in the hollows,
West wind sighs and rain is falling,
Thunder, lightning quickly follows.

Earth's still cold from winter sleeping,
Daffodils still sheathed like spears,
Snowdrops brown from early flowering,
Cold winds bite your nose and ears.

Through the turmoil of our springtime
New life struggles to exist,
Tadpoles frozen in their jelly,
Small lambs born in snow and mist.

Yet on straw bonnets flowers cluster,
New leaves twine and ribbons coil.
Nestling safe in coloured boxes,
Chocolate eggs, encased in foil.

And saffron biscuits, fruit-encrusted,
Are big enough to fill your hand,
Simnel cakes all almond-pasted,
Ringed with eggs and oven-tanned.

We who long for warmth and comfort
Of the summer's golden days,

See new life and hope at Easter,
A new beginning, God be praised.

## Donkey waiting

Dumb creature, with your panting bellow,
Long ears, rough coat, a stubborn fellow.
Many men have used you ill,
And kick you and abuse you still.

Yet patiently for him you wait:
Once more you will fulfill your fate,
And carry Christ the Lord again,
Triumphant to Jerusalem.

## Reading

### *Mark 11: 7–10*

They brought the colt to Jesus, threw their cloaks over the animal, and Jesus got on.
Many people spread their cloaks on the road, while others cut branches in the fields and spread them on the road. The people who were in front and those who followed behind began to shout, 'Praise God! God bless him who comes in the name of the Lord! God bless the coming kingdom of King David, our father! Praise God!'

## Prayers

Dear God,
We thank you for all of the precious animals that you have brought into your wonderful world. Help us to remember that they all have their own ways of living, and help us to try to understand them.
Amen.

Jesus riding on a donkey,
People shouting in the street.
Onward through the busy city,
Palm leaves strewn beneath his feet.

Where you lead us we will follow,
Do what you will ask us, Lord,

Follow Jesus when he calls us,
And his love is our reward.
Amen.

## End of the Assembly

## Follow-up classwork

Make an Easter bonnet and cover it with spring flowers, either fresh or cut from paper.

Make a collection of spring flowers and leaves for the nature table.

Forsythia and horse chestnut are among some of the twigs that will flower and leaf when brought indoors.

Make a cardboard-box theatre. Cut out characters from card and stick them onto thin dowel with plasticine.

## Further reading

**Acrobat Hamster** M. Cockett (Hamish Hamilton)
**Hare and the Easter Eggs** A. Uttley (Collins)
**Donkey Tales** D. Rush (Faber)
**Little Donkey's Big Day** Little Fish Books (Scripture Union)

ASSEMBLY 11

# At the zoo

## (Noah's ark)
*(Genesis 6–9)*

---

This Assembly is designed to introduce the story of Noah to children. It is hoped that in subsequent classroom work, various concepts can be discussed. These are:

The variety and beauty of life around us.

God's care for animals, and how we too can care for them, with emphasis on protection of wildlife and care of our pets.

God's care for people – how he rewards, forgives and keeps his promise.

How the family care for each other, play and learn together (the common theme of the 'Grandma and Katie' stories).

## Hymns and songs

**Things I love** (*1*) Come and Sing (*Scripture Union*)
**Animal sounds** (*7*) Come and Sing (*Scripture Union*)
**Noah was safe** (*51*) Come and Sing
**Just to show he cared** (*11*) Come and Sing Some More
**Stand up, clap hands** (*16*) Come and Sing Some More
**The butterfly song** (*27*) Come and Sing Some More
**Sing a rainbow** (*5*) Apusskidu (*Black*)
**The animals went in two by two** (*38*) Apusskidu
**Going to the Zoo** (*39*) Come and Praise (*BBC*)
**Have you heard the raindrops** (*2*) Come and Praise
**Who put the colours in the rainbow** (*12*) Come and Praise
**Who built the Ark** (*44*) Someone's Singing, Lord (*Black*)
**Going to the Zoo** (*Tom Paxton*) Seeing and Doing (*Thames TV*)

## Read the story

# At the zoo

On Alexander's second birthday, Grandma took everyone to the zoo for a treat. They all piled into the back of Grandma's car in the drizzle – Katie, Alexander, and their mum, Auntie Susan and Jenny. As they splashed off through the puddles, Grandma said, 'I do hope this rain stops soon.'

'It's all right, Grandma,' said Katie, 'I've got my wellies on and so have Alex and Jenny.'

The three children all stretched their legs out in front of them to show off their brightly coloured boots.

'And we've all got raincoats in the back,' added Mum.

'Well, that's all right, then,' smiled Grandma, and they all started to sing "Grandma's taking us to the zoo today". It was going to take more than a shower of rain to spoil the day, she thought, and by the time they had arrived at the zoo, the sun was struggling through the clouds.

While Grandma bought the tickets, the children ran on into the zoo. Right by the entrance was a flower bed, freshly planted with beautiful summer flowers and little trees. Beyond were more flower beds leading to the first of the animal enclosures, and there were still teams of gardeners at work, planting flowers and clipping the grass.

'I think Bristol Zoo's the most beautiful zoo in the country,' said Grandma as she joined them.

'Oh, no, Grandma,' said Katie, 'It must be the most beautiful zoo in the whole world!'

'What shall we see first?' asked Mum.

'The lions,' said Katie, immediately.

'Fish!' shouted Alexander.

'He likes the fish,' said Katie.

'He likes the fish,' repeated Alexander.

Jenny just ran around shrieking with excitement.

'I don't think she knows what she wants,' smiled Auntie Susan.

They went to the lion cages first because they were closer, and stood and watched the big cats pacing around or sleepily watching the people from where they lay. Suddenly the big lion with the mane roared out at them. Alexander and Jenny both laughed and roared back at him, but Katie looked a bit worried.

'It's just that I don't like loud noises,' she said, pulling Grandma towards the gorilla house. Instead of looking at the gorillas from the outside, they went inside to watch them. It was dark and warm inside the gorilla house, and quite empty. There was thick glass instead of bars so that they could see the animals more clearly. Katie stood gazing at a huge gorilla who lay back as though he was in a deck chair.

'He's enormous,' she said in a whisper, 'He's even bigger than Grandpa!' She didn't notice that Alexander had come up behind her, and had heard what she'd said.

'Grandpa, Grandpa!' he shouted, running right up to the glass and banging on it.

'Don't be so silly,' said Katie, 'You know that isn't Grandpa. He's at work, isn't he, Grandma? Now, do be quiet, or you'll frighten the gorillas.'

Jenny came in just then, holding Auntie Susan's and Mum's hands. Another group of families followed them in, and soon the peace of the dark gorilla house was broken by the excited shouts of the children. The animals didn't seem too worried by the noise, and a little baby gorilla stared out curiously at all the people from its mother's arms.

As they left the gorilla house, the rain was starting again.

'I know,' called Grandma. 'The reptile house.' And she led the way through the rain with her umbrella up, holding Katie's hand.

Inside the reptile house it was hot and steamy. Banks of tropical plants lined the walls and behind the glass they could see snakes coiled.

Alexander went up to one of the larger cages and pressed his nose against the glass.

'Fish,' he said happily, pointing in.

'No, darling,' said Mum, 'not fish. Those are terrapins.'

'He likes the fish,' said Katie with a grin.

'He likes the fish,' repeated Alexander.

In the next cage a crocodile lay motionless, pretending to be a log.

'Fish,' said Alexander, pointing at it.

'That's a crocodile,' said Mum. 'He eats fish for dinner.'

'Dinner,' said Alexander. 'He likes dinner.'

'What a good idea,' said Grandma. But when they left the reptile house it was raining even harder than before.

'I know,' said Auntie Susan, 'there's a shelter by the lake. We can have our sandwiches there.'

As they ran through the rain, the children laughed and jumped into the puddles. Alexander found an overflowing gutter and stood underneath it, until his mum pulled him away.

'He's still very silly, even though he's two now,' said Katie. 'He doesn't seem to care if he gets wet or dirty, and he eats anything. I found him sucking a worm the other day.'

Grandma laughed.

'When you were his age, I found a beetle in your mouth,' she said. 'I don't know how long it had been there.'

'I think you must be wrong, Grandma,' said Katie, frowning, 'I'd never do anything as horrible as that.'

They all sat down under the shelter and opened their lunch boxes. As they ate, other families ran under the shelter to have their lunch in the dry. Soon there were a lot of children running about excitedly while their parents stared gloomily at the rain.

Grandma took Katie, Alexander and Jenny to the kiosk when they'd all finished their sandwiches.

'I'll buy you all a treat,' she said. 'How about an animal mask?'

Jenny immediately chose a lion mask, and Grandma popped it over her curls. Katie wanted a monkey mask, and Alexander became upset when he couldn't have a fish mask.

'I'm sorry, Alex,' said Grandma, 'But they don't do any fish masks. Wouldn't you like another sort?'

He pointed to Jenny's mask, so Grandma bought another lion and put it on him. He and Jenny ran back to the shelter roaring loudly. When the other children under the shelter saw the masks, they all wanted one, and very soon there were all sorts of animals running around. Little fights broke out as the children became over-excited.

'Shall we play a game?' asked Grandma.

'Yes, please,' said Auntie Susan. 'That should calm them down a bit.'

So Grandma got Katie, Jenny and Alexander to bang their hands on the wooden seat, then stamp their feet on the ground. Soon, some of the other children came to see what they were doing.

'It's a game,' said Katie. 'Would you like to join in?'

'What's it about?' asked a bigger boy.

'Well, it's about rain,' said Grandma, 'and animals, and a man called Noah. You can be Noah if you like.'

'All right,' said the boy, 'what do I do?'

'I want to be something as well,' said a girl.

'You can be Mrs Noah,' said Grandma. 'I'll tell you all what to say.'

The girl giggled, looking at the boy. Another boy wanted to join in, and Grandma said,

'You can be the voice of God.'

'What do I say?' asked the boy, and Grandma whispered in his ear.

He stood up on a bench and said, in a deep voice, 'Noah, this is God here. I want you to build a boat. It's going to rain very hard, but you and your family'll be safe in the boat.'

Then Grandma whispered to the boy playing Noah, and he said, 'Saw the wood and build a boat.'

All of the other children made sawing noises.

'Now hammer the nails,' said Noah, and the children pretended to hammer nails. By now, all the children in the shelter had joined in the game. When the boat had been built and painted, the voice of God said,

'Well done. You must call the boat the Ark. Put all the animals on board so they can be saved too.'

So Noah and Mrs Noah pretended to get on the Ark, and all of the children who had animal masks put them on. Noah and Mrs Noah held their arms high up so that the animals could walk underneath.

'Into the Ark,' they all chanted, 'It's going to rain.' And in went lions, tigers, monkeys and frogs. There were three children left who didn't have masks, so Grandma said,

'Put your raincoats over your heads and be elephants. Your arms can be the trunks.' So the three elephants went into the ark. When everyone was in the ark, Grandma said, 'Now the rain will start.'

She patted her legs with her hands to make the sound of the rain. All of the children did the same.

'Then it got harder,' and the patting got louder,

'Then harder still,' and the children stamped their feet.

'It was a downpour!' shouted Grandma, 'Then it stopped!'

Everybody stopped patting and stamping.

'The great Ark rocked backwards and forwards on the water,' said Grandma, as the children swayed to and fro.

Then the voice of God said, 'Noah, of all the people in the

whole world you were the only one who loved me and obeyed my word. You and your family and the animals have been saved. When the ground is dry, you can go and multiply and fill the earth.'

After a bit more rocking, the Ark stopped.

'We've landed on Mount Ararat,' said Noah after Grandma had whispered to him, 'All you animals can get out now.'

So all of the animals left the Ark under Noah and Mrs Noah's arms, and everybody clapped. All of the mothers and fathers, aunties and uncles, grandmas and grandpas had been watching and they all agreed that it had been a very fine game.

'And look,' said Auntie Susan, 'the sun's come out again.'

Everybody packed away their sandwiches and left the shelter to go back round the zoo. As they set off for the aquarium to please Alexander, Katie said, 'Grandma, why did Noah have to do sums?'

'What sums?' asked Grandma.

'You said he had to multiply,' said Katie.

'Oh, that just means to make more of your kind,' laughed Grandma. 'You know, like your Mummy and Daddy made you, and like the mummy and daddy gorilla made the little baby gorilla.'

'I see,' said Katie. 'I didn't think it was fair that Noah should have to do sums after he'd built the Ark.'

Alexander loved the aquarium. The fish tanks went right over the top of their heads so that they seemed to be walking under water. There were huge fish, as big as Alexander, and tiny fish that looked like swimming butterflies. Alexander wanted to stay there when the others were ready to leave.

'Come on,' said Mum, 'there are lots of other things to see.'

But Alexander wouldn't budge, and eventually he had to be carried out kicking and screaming, 'He likes the fish, he likes the fish!'

'You don't, you know,' said Mum. 'You just think you do. You wouldn't eat your fishcakes the other day.'

They decided to go and watch the seals being fed next. Alexander had calmed down a bit by the time they reached the seals' pool. The keeper came onto the poolside carrying a big bucket of fish, and all the seals got very excited.

The keeper started to throw the fish to the seals, and some of them were very good at catching them. Alexander was very interested. He realised what it was that the keeper was throwing.

'Fish,' he shouted. 'He *likes* the fish, he does, he does!'

The keeper threw one fish high up in the air, and a seal leapt up to catch it. But the fish bounced off the seal's nose and shot out of the pool to hit Grandma right in the face. Although she was very surprised, she caught the fish as it fell, and everyone laughed loudly, except for Alexander. He reached up and grabbed the fish from Grandma, and took a great bite from it.

It was horrible! He threw it down to the ground and spat. Mum picked up the bitten fish and threw it back into the pool.

'Doesn't like the fish,' said Alexander, and pulled his mask down firmly over his face.

'I didn't think you would,' said Mum.

As they were leaving, Katie said to Grandma, 'It was a lovely day, Grandma. I did enjoy the story about Noah and the Ark. Do you think we'll have to build an Ark if it carries on raining?'

'No,' said Grandma. 'After God saved Noah from the flood he promised never to send another flood to destroy the world. To give a sign of his promise, he put the first rainbow in the sky, so that Noah would always remember.'

'There's a bit of a rainbow over there,' said Katie, pointing to a patch of sky. 'I'm glad we don't have to build another Ark. My arm's still tired from sawing wood for the last one.'

## Poems

### At the zoo

Monkeys gathered in damp huddles
Watch the children jump in puddles.
Parents' plans are all in muddles,
Walking round the zoo.

Parrots feathers dripping wet,
Penguins soaked as they can get.
There's never been so much rain, I'll bet,
Falling on the zoo.

But the rain will soon have passed.
Mum says storms like this don't last

And the sun will come out fast,
Shining on the zoo.

Then we'll see the zebras run,
Tigers stretching in the sun,
Us and them all having fun,
Happy in the zoo.

## Rainbow beyond my reach

Knee-deep in long, wet grass I stood,
In the lane beside the wood.
As the glowering storm clouds cleared,
A shaft of vibrant light appeared;
Light that bent into a bow
And showered on the fields below,
Colours from a painter's brush
That touched each twig and singing thrush.

Raindrops caught the shining light
On storm-wet leaves and buds curled tight.
Yet I could not touch the bands
Growing beyond my outstretched hands;
But still I chased the rainbow's gleam,
Into the fields and over streams,
Vanishing as I ran the race,

Appearing in another place
Beyond my reach.

(Can you find the acrostic in the second verse? The first letters of each line are the same as the initial letters of the colours of the rainbow.)

## Reading

### *2 Samuel 23: 3–5*

The God of Israel has spoken;
the protector of Israel said to me:
'The king who rules with justice,
who rules in obedience to God,
is like the sun shining on a cloudless dawn,
the sun that makes the grass sparkle after rain.'

And that is how God will bless my descendants,
because he has made an eternal covenant with me,
an agreement that will not be broken,
a promise that will not be changed.

## Prayer

Slugs and snails, moths and mice,
Worms and snakes and fat woodlice,
Earwigs, wasps and spiders small,
Help me, God, to love them all.
Amen.

## End of the Assembly

## Follow-up classwork

Visit a zoo or animal reserve.

Make animal masks.

Dramatise the story of Noah's Ark.

Make storm music – drumming fingers, glockenspiel and chime bars for rain, shakers and maracas for heavy rain and hail, drums and shaken card for thunder, cymbals for lightning.

Measure the Ark – make a chalk outline; the Ark was 300 cubits long, 50 cubits wide and 30 cubits high, a cubit being about 20 inches (18–22 in.).

## Further reading

**At the Zoo** P. Usborne (Macdonald)
**The Zoo Keeper** Anne Stewart (Hamish Hamilton)
**Zoo Animals in Colour** C. Kilpatrick (Octopus)
**Flash, Crash, Rumble and Roll** F. M. Branley (Black)
**It's Raining** L. Bolwell (Wayland)
**Weatherwatch** A. Ford (Methuen Walker)
**'Ark' stories** J. Ryan (Hamlyn)
**Two By Two** Little Fish Books (Scripture Union)

ASSEMBLY 12

# The butterfly watch

## (The parable of the talents)
*Matthew 25: 14–30 and Luke 19: 12–27*

---

This story introduces the Parable of the Talents (also known as the Parable of the Pounds). The themes it is hoped will be discussed are:

Using your 'talents' (abilities, skills) to their best effect.
Sharing.
Appreciating gifts and not wasting them.

## Hymns and songs

**Butterflies** (*22*) Knock at the Door (*Ward Lock*)
**Ticking Clocks** (*25*) Flying a Round (*Black*)

## Read the story

## The butterfly watch

Grandma and Grandpa had gone on holiday to see Katie's cousin Lucy and her mum and dad, who lived in a boat in Gibraltar. When they came back, all brown from the sun, they came to see Katie and her family. Auntie Susan and Katie's cousin Jenny were visiting that day, as well, and Grandma and Grandpa had brought presents for all of the children.

Katie's little brother Alexander and Jenny both had soft toy monkeys and a big bag of chocolate buttons. Katie had a bag of sweets that looked just like seaside pebbles and a beautiful watch with a butterfly on it. The butterfly's antennae were the hands of the watch and pointed to the right time. Katie was delighted with it.

Mum put the watch on to Katie's wrist while the two little children were eating some of their chocolate buttons.

'It's lovely, Grandma,' said Katie, holding her wrist up and admiring it. 'Thank you ever so much.'

She went up to Grandma and Grandpa and gave them both a big kiss.

It was a lovely sunny day and all the family were sitting outside in garden chairs. The three children were all playing happily in the sand pit and the paddling pool when suddenly there was a squawking and fluttering from the glass conservatory by the house.

Cosmo the black and white cat had caught a bird and taken it indoors to hide it from the people. He knew that they would take it away from him if they could. But the bird had escaped from his claws and was fluttering around against the glass, trying to get out. Mum jumped to her feet and ran into the conservatory. She grabbed the cat and held him while Katie's dad opened the windows wide. Within a few minutes, the frightened bird had found his way back outside and flown into a nearby tree where he sat, chirping loudly and fluffing out his feathers.

Katie followed Mum as she carried Cosmo out into the garden. Cosmo hung limply from her arms, and when he was put on the ground he slunk under a hedge and sat there sulking. He knew that he had done wrong but he kept an eye open for the bird, sitting far above him.

'Cosmo, that's very naughty,' scolded Katie. 'You'll get a smack if you catch birds again. Tell him not to, Grandpa.'

'I'm afraid that wouldn't do any good, Katie,' said Grandpa. 'It's a cat's nature to catch birds.'

'I'll make a cup of tea after all that excitement,' said Dad, 'or would anyone prefer coffee?'

'No, tea will be fine,' said Grandpa, 'I'll give you a hand.'

'Let's have another chocolate button,' said Auntie Susan, and little Jenny came running up from the hedge where she and Alexander had been watching Cosmo sulk. But nobody could find the chocolates.

'Where are they, Jenny?' asked Auntie Susan.

'Sandy eat,' said Jenny, pointing to Alexander who had wandered over to the water again. He had his back to everybody.

'Oh no,' said Katie, 'Alex got all of the buttons while we were watching the cat!'

Alexander's cheeks were bulging with chocolate, and his face was brown. In the paddling pool they could see the two monkeys floating around, and on the bottom lay the pebble sweets. They looked even more real under the water. Alexander picked up a spade and tried to sink the monkeys with it.

'It's no good trying to hide them,' said Mum. 'Come on, I'm going to take those chocolate buttons out of your mouth before you choke.'

She picked him up and carried him off into the house, followed by Jenny, who was delighted that it hadn't been she who was naughty this time. Auntie Susan fished out the pebble sweets and put them on the table to dry.

'They'll be as good as new in a while,' she said, and went to peg out the monkeys by their ears on the washing line.

'It's not fair,' said Katie, 'Alex takes all of my things when I'm not looking.'

'He's too little to understand that he shouldn't,' said Grandma. 'When he gets a bit older he'll realise that he mustn't touch your toys.'

'Well I can't wait till then,' said Katie, pouting. 'I'll have nothing left. I get really fed up with him.'

Mum came back out with Alexander and Jenny. Alexander had a big smile on his face. He had managed to eat quite a lot of the buttons while his mum was getting them out of his cheeks.

Dad and Grandpa came out of the house after a while carrying a tray of tea and the biscuit tin. Everyone sat in the sun and listened to Grandma and Grandpa talking about their holiday. They had really enjoyed themselves. They got out loads of photographs and started talking about rocks and plants. After a few minutes, Katie got a bit bored and wandered off up the garden. She came back a bit later with a secret smile on her face.

Mum was the first one to notice that Katie wasn't wearing her new watch.

'Katie, what have you done with your lovely butterfly watch?' she asked.

'I've hidden it,' she said.

'Why on earth would you want to do that?' asked Mum.

'So that Alexander can't get it and break it,' said Katie.

'Don't be silly, Katie,' said her dad. 'Go and get your watch and put it back on. It'll get lost.'

'No it won't,' answered Katie. 'I know just where it is. I'll go and get it when Alexander's a bit older.'

'But it'll get wet,' said Grandma.

'No it won't,' said Katie, even more firmly than before, 'because I've wrapped it up in the bag the chocolate drops were in. Before *he* ate them.'

'Katie, get your watch right now,' said Mum.
'No!' said Katie. She put her hands over her ears and closed her eyes tightly. Her lips were pressed together hard and she went stamping off on her own.
'Well, it's time for us to be off,' said Auntie Susan. 'I must get tea ready for Jenny and her dad.'
'Yes, it's almost time for Alexander's bath now,' said Mum, 'I'll take him up now and leave Katie with her grandma. See you on Saturday.'
Auntie Susan and Jenny went home and Dad and Grandpa tidied up the toys. Katie came up to Grandma and said, 'Can I come and sit on your lap?'
'Of course you can,' said Grandma. 'Katie, you do like your watch, don't you?'
'Oh, yes, Grandma, it's ever so nice. I just want to keep it safe.'
'Aren't you worried that someone might step on it and break it?'
'No one can step on it,' said Katie. 'It's well hidden.'
'It's a pity you're not wearing it,' said Grandma. 'I had a surprise planned for your bed time.'
'Is the surprise about my watch?' asked Katie.
'Yes,' said Grandma. 'Don't you want to go and get it?'
Katie just shook her head and put her thumb in her mouth.
'Well, shall I tell you a story instead?' asked Grandma.
Katie nodded and smiled around her thumb.
'This is a story that Jesus told,' said Grandma.
'Is it a story about Jesus' watch?' asked Katie.
'No,' said Grandma, smiling, 'Jesus didn't have a watch. Nobody had a watch in those days. They hadn't been invented. This is a story about a man who had three servants. The man had to go away on a long trip, so he called his servants and gave them all some money to look after. He gave the first servant five coins, he gave the second servant two coins and he gave the third servant one coin.'
'Was it pennies, Grandma?' asked Katie.
'No, these were big coins, worth quite a lot. The man wanted his servants to look after the money while he was away. When he had gone, the first servant went out and used the money to buy and sell things. He did very well, and soon had another five coins to add to the first five.'
'He had ten coins,' said Katie.
'Yes, that's right. That's very good,' said Grandma. 'Well,

the second servant did the same thing, and he doubled his two coins to four coins.'

'I bet the other servant did that too,' said Katie.

'No, he didn't,' said Grandma, 'In fact, the third servant went off to a secret place and buried his money in the ground to keep it safe. When their master came home again, he called his servants in and asked them what they had done with the money he had left them.

'The first servant told his master that he had used the five coins to trade with and had doubled them. The second servant also said that he had doubled the money he had been left with. The man was very pleased. He told the two servants that, since they could be trusted to look after small sums of money, he would put them in charge of all of his money. Then he asked the third servant what he had done with the coin that he had been left with.

'The servant told his master that he had kept the money safe by hiding it in the ground. He said that he was afraid of his master's anger if he had lost any of the money by trading with it.

'The master was very angry. He said that it was stupid to worry about what might happen to the money. After all, the servant could have put the money in the bank and at least it would have earned some interest.'

'What's interest?' asked Katie.

'It's what a bank pays you to save your money with them,' answered Grandma. 'The master was angry because the servant had been too lazy to bother using the money properly. He took the money away from him and gave it to one of the other servants, and threw the third servant out of his house.'

Katie took her thumb out of her mouth and sat up.

'What does it mean, Grandma?'

'I think Jesus might have been telling us that we can't just hide things away to keep them safe. We should use them, and make the most of them,' said Grandma.

'If you put money in the ground it would go a funny colour,' said Katie. 'Mum found an old penny yesterday when she was digging the garden. It was all green and horrible.'

'Yes,' replied Grandma, 'and if you put paper money into the ground it might get nibbled up by mice.'

'Do mice nibble all sorts of paper?' asked Katie in a worried voice, looking down the garden.

'Especially paper with traces of food on,' said Grandma.

'Like chocolate, you mean?' said Katie.
'Mice love chocolate,' said Grandma.
Katie jumped off Grandma's lap and pulled at her hand.
'Quick, Grandma, I'll show you where I buried the watch and we can get it back before the mice find it,' she said.
They went down the garden to the bushes at the end.
'It was under this one,' said Katie, pointing at the soil. 'I'm sure this was the one.'
She scrabbled at the soil, but no chocolate button bag appeared.
'No, I think it was this one,' she said, as she searched under another bush. The watch was nowhere to be found.
'Oh, Grandma, I can't remember which one I hid it under!' she cried. 'The mice will get it!'
Grandma looked at her watch.
'Just a minute.' she said. 'If you keep quiet, the watch will soon tell us where it is.'
'How can it do that?' said Katie, brightening up a bit.
'Wait and see,' said Grandma, still looking at her watch.
They both stood there quietly, Katie holding her breath in suspense. After a little while, they heard a tiny tune playing, like a little music box far away. They followed the sound to a bush, and Katie bent down and dug with her fingers until she finally held up a grubby chocolate button bag.
'It's here, Grandma!' she said. 'It told us where it was. It's magic!'
'No, not magic,' smiled Grandma. 'That's your special surprise. The watch plays a tune when it's your bed time.'
'I'm glad I got it back from under the bush,' said Katie. 'Even if Alex does get it sometimes, it would be dreadful to have missed the beautiful music. I'm going to wear it all day and put it somewhere safe when I go to bed. It's the most wonderful watch in the world.'
Katie put the watch back on her wrist and looked at the butterfly on it. The butterfly's antennae told her that it was getting late, and in a few moments she heard her mum calling from the house, 'Bath time, Katie.'
'Don't forget to take it off before you get in the bath,' called Grandma as Katie ran down the garden path. 'I don't think butterflies can swim.'

# Poems

## Time

Face without a nose or eyes,
Eyebrows, chin or lips.
Hands without a palm or wrist,
Nails or finger tips.

Leather strap and buckle bright,
Digital display
Of liquid crystal, glowing clear,
To mark the time of day.

Winding spring and balance wheel,
Alarms that buzz or chime.
In my pocket, on my wrist,
My watch tells me the time.

## Hide and seek

'It's your turn to be On It, kid.'
On what? An egg? I'm not a hen.
'No, you can count and we will hide.'
What shall I count up to? Ten?

'No, count to sixty – if you can.'
I could count a million tens.
But I agreed to count out loud
To sixty, and to find them then.

I must close my eyes and count.
What comes after twenty three?
What's this fungus I can feel,
Like a soft ear on the tree?

There's an ant upon the trunk,
Close to where my elbow bends,
Scurrying round the pitted bark
And carrying an injured friend.

'We're ready!' comes a distant shout,
And, as I open my left eye,

An eau-de-nil grub drops its line
Of silken thread, and sails on by.

Was it twenty three I'd said?
A toad crawls round the elder's bole
And makes towards the nearby brook,
The cool damp stones and roots his goal.

If I should hide between the reeds
To watch the minnows' pebbly lair,
And damsel flies inflate their wings,
Nobody would know I'm there.

They came and shouted, 'Where's that kid?
I knew we shouldn't let him play.'
I lay amongst the willow herb
And very soon they went away.

## Reading

### *Extract from Ecclesiastes 3:1–8*

To everything there is a season,
And a time to every purpose under Heaven:
A time to be born, and a time to die;
A time to plant, and a time to harvest;
A time to kill, and a time to heal;
A time to weep, and a time to laugh;
A time to mourn, and a time to dance;
A time to get, and a time to lose;
A time to keep, and a time to cast away.

## Prayers

I saw a butterfly today.
Dear God, you gave it glorious wings;
It closed them once, then flew away.
What wondrous sights the Summer brings!

The caterpillar, small and plump,
Is busy eating, changing skins;
The pupa on the old tree stump
Keeps still until new life begins.

We thank you for the mystery
Of all your creatures here below,
Your care of them, that we can see
How beautiful we all might grow.
Amen.

You gave us talents, Lord;
The gifts to heal, to care, to love, to entertain,
Or simply to enjoy your beautiful world.
Everyone can do something well in their life.
Help us to use our gifts wisely,
In your name,
Amen.

## End of the Assembly

## Follow-up classwork

Using your talents: Can you sing a song, dance, do an impression of a famous person, recite a poem or nursery rhyme, make a picture, play a musical instrument?

Are you good with numbers?

Can you cook?

Do you have an interest in nature, prehistoric animals, knights, castles, stamps or sport?

Are you good at caring for others?

Do you look after your friends and family? Say what you do.

Do you help to collect aid for those people who are starving; the people in hospital; the people who are poor?

Tell about the people who need your help.

Do you look after the countryside? Say how you help to take care of our beautiful land.

Visit a butterfly farm. Keep chrysalids in a home-made vivarium, watch them hatch. Make models of butterflies; give them symmetrically patterned wings.

## Further reading

**The Butterfly Collector** F. Testa & N. Lewis (Andersen Press)
**The Lost and Found House** C. Joerns (Collins)

ASSEMBLY 13

# Katie swimming

## (Jesus walking on the water)
*Matthew 14:22–33, Mark 6:45–52 and John 6:15–21*

---

This Assembly introduces the story of Jesus walking on the water. It shows us that, with faith, all sorts of difficulties can be overcome, and that we can do things we thought impossible. Themes that can be discussed in classroom follow-up are:

Being brave,
Having faith – both in God and in our own abilities.

## Hymns and songs

**Peter's Brown Boat** (*27*) Come and Sing (*Scripture Union*)
**In Galilee Beside The Sea** (*28*) Come and Sing
**Now Jesus One Day** (*30*) Someone's Singing, Lord (*Black*)
**Place To Be** (*34*) Tinderbox (*Black*)
**Can You Walk On Tiptoe?** (*p14*) Ten Galloping Horses (*Warne*)

## Read the story

## Katie swimming

'Alexander swam across the pool today,' said Katie's mum.

Katie looked surprised.

'All by himself?' she asked.

'Yes,' said Mum. 'All by himself, with his arm bands on.'

'Well, aren't you a clever boy!' said Katie, crouching down to be level with Alexander, who was playing with some toy cars. He smiled happily.

'Yes, clever,' he said.

'Katie, *you* haven't been swimming since last summer, have you?' said Mum. 'I think it's about time we took you to the swimming pool again, don't you?'

'Oh, I've had a cold,' said Katie in a very off-hand way.

'That was weeks ago,' said Mum. 'Don't worry, you'll love the pool.'

Two days later, Mum and Grandma met Katie from school. They had Alexander with them.

'I thought we'd go swimming today,' said Mum.

'Oh, no, not today,' said Katie. 'I wanted to go to Georgina's house to play. Can't we make it another day?'

'No,' said Mum firmly, 'Today's the only day that Grandma can come with us, and I need her to look after one of you while I look after the other one. Anyway, I've got all our costumes and towels with me. Come along, you'll have a lovely time.'

So they all walked off to the swimming pool. Grandma and Katie walked together and Katie held Grandma's hand without being asked to. Grandma told Katie about how she had learned to swim when she was a very young girl.

'Not as young as me, I don't expect?' asked Katie.

'Why, I was younger than you,' said Grandma, and went on to tell Katie about her knitted costume that had stretched when it got wet.

'It became so large that I could hardly keep it on,' said Grandma. They laughed about that all the way to the pool.

After buying their tickets, they walked down the long flight of stairs that led to the changing rooms. Katie sniffed.

'What's that funny smell?' she complained. 'I don't like it.'

'That's just the chlorine,' explained Mum. 'It's put into the water to keep it clean. Don't worry, in a few minutes you won't notice it at all.'

While Mum changed Alexander, Grandma helped Katie into her shiny pink swimming costume and pink armbands. Katie looked at Alex in his red armbands and his smart black trunks. He had a little blue and white badge on the trunks.

'What's the badge?' she asked. 'I haven't seen it before.'

'He got that for swimming across the baths,' said Mum proudly.

Katie looked down at her plain pink costume. She went to Grandma and held her hand. When they were all ready, they went to the pool.

It looked lovely. The water sparkled from the sun that shone through the huge windows. There were quite a few people swimming, the adults at the deeper end, and the children splashing around in the shallows. The noise of their laughter echoed from the high ceiling.

Mum climbed into the pool while Grandma held Alexander

and Katie by their hands. Then Alex went to the side of the pool, curled his little toes over the edge, and, when Mum was ready, leapt towards her. He landed with a huge splash in the pool and bobbed up right in front of her.

'Good boy,' said Mum.

Alexander was very pleased with himself.

'I'll get in first and help you in, shall I?' asked Grandma to Katie.

'I don't think I'll bother getting into the water today,' said Katie. 'It's too cold.'

'Oh, no, it's not, young lady,' said Mum, 'it's lovely. I don't know what all the fuss is about. Now, do hurry up and get in.'

But Katie turned and started to run back to the changing rooms.

'Would you please get her, Grandma?' said Mum.

Before she got to the changing rooms Katie slipped on the wet floor and landed heavily on her bottom. You can guess that Katie made a lot of noise and that Grandma had to take her back to the changing rooms quickly before everyone got a headache.

When Mum and Alexander had finished swimming they found Katie sitting with Grandma in the snack bar. 'Silly girl,' said Mum. 'One of the most important rules of swimming is "I must not run".'

'I know,' said Katie, 'Grandma has told me, lots of times. You know, I'd rather watch than be down there in the water. It looks quite nice from up here.'

Grandma phoned Katie's mum later that evening.

'What did Grandma say?' asked Katie. 'I heard you talk about a party.'

'Yes, that's right,' said Mum. 'Grandma is going to have a swimming party for you and some of your friends. Would you like that?'

Katie was a bit doubtful.

'Well, I do like parties,' she said, 'but I hate swimming.'

Grandma had been a teacher before she had retired, and her old school had an indoor swimming pool that she could hire for an hour one evening a week. The pool was quite small, and shallow enough so that even the shortest child could stand up easily in it. Grandma and Mum talked to the mothers of Katie's friends on the telephone, and asked if they would like to go to a special swimming party once a week for the next few weeks.

Most of the mums were very pleased to have the chance to take their children swimming in a small pool, and there were soon enough children going to cover the cost of hiring the pool.

When the day for the swimming party came, all of the children and their mums met at the pool after school. Katie didn't know if she was looking forward to the party or not, but when she saw how small the pool was, she felt better. The water looked very blue and inviting.

The children were soon all changed, and had put on their arm bands. Grandma was already waiting for them in the water, and Georgina was the first to walk down the shallow steps into the pool.

'Ooh, it's lovely and warm!' she shouted, and all the rest of the children followed her in. Even Katie.

Soon, everyone was jumping and splashing around. Some children still stayed close to the edge of the pool and held their mother's hands, but it wasn't long before they all joined in. It was so shallow that they all felt quite safe.

'Can we play party games now, Grandma?' asked Katie, who was trying very hard not to let any of her friends see that she didn't like getting her face wet.

'Right,' said Grandma. 'Listen, everybody, we're going to play some swimming party games now.'

Everyone cheered. One of the mothers handed out round polystyrene floats while Grandma went on, 'I want you all to pretend that you're driving a dirty old lorry up a hill. The float can be your steering wheel. You can make the lorry noises yourselves.'

The children all walked around in the water making lorry noises, holding the floats out in front of them the way that Grandma showed them.

'Stop!' called Grandma. 'Now you're driving a fast sports car. Be careful not to hit anyone.'

Everyone went as fast as they could through the water, making sports car noises and turning their wheels. Water splashed and they got very excited.

'Stop!' called Grandma. 'Right, now keep holding your floats and park your cars. You are all going to be big bouncing rubber balls. I want to see who can bounce the highest.'

All the rubber balls bounced and splashed until the water started to go over the sides and splash some of the mothers.

'Stop!' called Grandma. 'Now you are still going to bounce,

but now you're going to be animals that bounce around Australia.'

'Kangaroos!' shouted some of the children.

'That's right,' said Grandma. 'And kangaroos bounce with their feet together. Off you go.'

The pool was full of kangaroos, bouncing and splashing.

'That's enough now,' called Grandma. 'You don't want to get too tired. Now you are all going to wear a pair of invisible seven league boots. Those are magic boots that let you take enormous steps.'

So everyone pretended to put on their invisible seven league boots, and walked around the pool, holding on to their floats, taking huge steps.

After that, Grandma showed them how to be crocodiles, hippopotamuses and submarines. Everyone enjoyed themselves, and even Katie was having a good time. She had forgotten about being afraid of the water. The pool was warm and shallow, and she knew nothing nasty could happen to her. Besides, all of her friends were there with her.

All too soon, their hour was up and it was time to get dressed and go home. But, as Grandma reminded them all, they could do it all over again next week.

'Hooray,' shouted the children.

Six weeks later, all of the children were happy and confident in the water. Most of them could be submarines, with their faces right in the water, and even Katie had forgotten that she was ever afraid. But then it was time for the pool to be closed for a while for cleaning, and Grandma had to explain to the children that their swimming parties were finished.

'But now that you are all so good in the water, your mummies and daddies can take you to the big pool,' she said.

The next week, Grandma met Katie after school, to take her to the big pool. Alexander was staying at home with his mum because he had a bad cough. But on the way down to the changing rooms, Katie stopped.

'What's the matter, darling?' asked Grandma, putting her arm round Katie's shoulders.

'Oh, Grandma,' wailed Katie, 'I'm still frightened. It's so deep.'

'Don't be scared,' said Grandma. 'Let's go to the snack bar for a while and watch the swimmers. I'll tell you a story about the water.'

So they went and sat in the snack bar, and Grandma bought

them both orange juice. Katie blew her nose on Grandma's handkerchief, and Grandma told her the story.

'A long time ago,' said Grandma, 'when Jesus was a grown up man, he had been talking to a crowd of people beside a big lake called the Sea of Galilee. When he had finished, he was very tired, and decided to go into the mountains to pray. He told his friends to get into their boat and go across the lake, and he would meet them on the other side.

'But during the night, a wind blew up, and the ship was stuck in the middle of the water, being tossed around like a cork.

'At about three o'clock in the morning, Jesus came down from the mountain, and stepped onto the water.'

'What do you mean?' asked Katie. 'Did he swim?'

'No,' said Grandma, 'He walked right on top of the water.'

'Gosh,' breathed Katie.

'He walked on the lake, until he came near to his friends' boat. But when they saw him, walking like that, they were scared, and thought that they were seeing a ghost.'

'I'm not surprised,' said Katie.

'But Jesus called out, "Don't worry, it's me. Don't be afraid".'

'Jesus' friend, Peter, said, "Lord, if it's really you, tell me to come to you across the water." So Jesus told him to come. Peter stepped out of the ship, and found that he, too, could walk on the water, so he started to walk over to Jesus.

'But when Peter felt the force of the wind, he became afraid, and started to sink. He called out to Jesus, "Help, Lord, save me!" Jesus immediately put out his hand and caught Peter. He said, "You should have more faith in me. Why did you doubt?" and helped Peter safely into the boat.

'If Peter had had more faith, he would have been able to walk on the water with Jesus.'

'Could Jesus have made me walk on the water?' asked Katie.

'Well, I should think so,' said Grandma, 'if you had been in the boat with Peter, and had enough faith.'

'Could he make me fly?' asked Katie.

'Now, come on, Katie,' said Grandma. 'You know that God made birds and butterflies to fly. But he made man clever enough to invent aeroplanes to fly in. The story is to show you that you must trust in Jesus and have faith. If you do, then you can do all sorts of things. Even things that you thought were impossible.'

'You mean, like swimming?' asked Katie.

'Yes, I do,' said Grandma. 'You know how to enjoy yourself in the water. Now you must have enough faith to believe that you can do the same in this pool, even though you thought it was too deep.'

'You'll keep me safe, won't you, Grandma?' asked Katie, in a small voice.

'Yes, darling, I will. Just like Jesus kept Peter safe. Now, are you ready?'

'I'm ready,' said Katie, and she and Grandma walked down the stairs to the changing rooms.

## Poems

### Swimming

I long to swim through fields of grass,
That gleams and bends like new-washed hair;
I long to swim through blossom fall,
That crowds the almond-scented air.

I long to swim through autumn mists,
Where woodsmoke threads reach to the sky;
I long to swim through falling snow,
As noiseless as a robin's sigh.

If I were butterfly or bird,
I'd soar and swoop and float with ease,
But without wings, I sadly swim
In chlorined pools and crowded seas.

### Learning to swim

We learned to swim some years ago,
Me and my sister, after school.
The waves beat in against the rocks
And rippled in the tidal pools.

In masks and snorkels we would stoop
To closely scan the weedy lairs
Of crabs and creatures small and strange,
That dodged each others' traps and snares.

We watched the banks of seaweed sway,
Like red and olive tangled trees.
Bent over, rapt, we scarcely felt
The moment when we floated free.

## Reading

## Jesus walking on the water

### *Matthew 14: 24–27 and 33*

. . . by this time the boat was far out in the lake, tossed about by the waves, because the wind was blowing against it.
Between three and six o'clock in the morning Jesus came to the disciples, walking on the water.
When they saw him walking on the water, they were terrified. 'It's a ghost!' they said, and screamed with fear.

Jesus spoke to them at once.
'Courage!' he said, 'It is I. Don't be afraid!'

Then the disciples in the boat worshipped Jesus. 'Truly you are the Son of God!' they exclaimed.

## Prayers

Oh, God, who knowest us to be set in the midst of so many and great dangers, that by reason of the frailty of our nature we cannot always stand upright; grant to us such strength and protection, as may support us in all dangers, and carry us through all temptations; through Jesus Christ our Lord. Amen.

*The Book Of Common Prayer*

Dear God,
There is nothing we cannot do with your love to guide us.
No task will be too hard, no effort too demanding,
If we do things in your name.
Give us the courage to go on when the way seems difficult.
We know that you are beside us.
Amen.

## End of the Assembly

## Follow-up classwork

Look at safety in the swimming pool first. Fixed rules are; No running at any time, no pushing or shouting. Flotation aids, getting into the water safely, knowing the safety signal (eg a whistle which will only be used in an emergency).

Water familiarisation in a learners' pool – wear arm bands, hold a float with your arms out straight, walk to all parts of the pool.

Exercises:

(i) Holding the float, use it as the steering wheel of a lorry; drive the lorry.
(ii) Drive a sports car.
(iii) Be a bouncing ball.
(iv) Be a kangaroo.
(v) Wearing seven-league boots, stride around the pool.
(vi) Be a crocodile with your chin on the float.
(vii) Be a hippopotamus with your nose on the float.
(viii) Be a paddle steamer, kicking your legs to make a splash.
(ix) Be a submarine, head down, making small leg-kicks.

Look at fishermen and the work of the R.N.L.I.

Look at freshwater and salt water fish.

## Further reading

**My First Day At The Swimming Pool** W. Smith (Hutchinson)
**Jenny Learns To Swim** N. Snell (Hamilton)
**No Swimming For Sam** T. Lambert (Gazelle)

ASSEMBLY 14

# Alexander's fish

## (Jonah and the big fish)
*Jonah 1: 1–17 and 2: 1–10*

---

This Assembly introduces the story of Jonah. It tells us that Jonah chose not to listen to the word of God. He suffered, repented and was saved. Like Jonah we have a choice.

The children could be asked these questions:
Why should we listen to God's word?
How does God speak to us?
What does he say?
Who tells us what is wrong and what is right?
(Parents, church leaders, teachers, the Bible.)

## Hymns and songs

**When Lamps are Lighted in the Town** (*26*) Someone's Singing Lord (*Black*)
**I Listen and I Listen** (*60*) Come and Praise (*BBC*)
**God Made the Shore** (*4*) Come and Sing (*Scripture Union*)
**Jesus Knows** (*39*) Come and Sing
**Jonah** (*50*) Come and Sing
**Place to Be** (*34*) Tinder Box (*Black*)
**Come Listen to my Tale of Jonah** (*30*) Junior Praise (*Marshall Pickering*)

## Read the story

## Alexander's fish

(Have a sock puppet ready for Grandma's story.)
Mum and Dad had taken Katie and Alexander to the seaside for a holiday. It was the first time that Alexander had ever seen the sea, and he loved it. He spent hours splashing and playing in the shallow water, until Mum finally dragged him out, his little fingers all wrinkled, to have something to eat. Katie didn't like getting wet, but she liked to play just beyond the reach of the tide, digging holes and channels for the waves

to fill. She built roads and castles with moats, and decorated them with shells and bits of seaweed.

Both the children were enjoying themselves in their own way, while Mum and Dad looked after them, played with them and got food and dry towels ready for them.

When Grandma and Grandpa arrived for a day visit, both children were running around on the beach. They were wearing sun hats and bathing costumes, and Mum had rubbed some cream on their arms and legs so that they didn't burn in the hot sunshine.

Dad had put up the big striped umbrella to give them all somewhere shady to sit, and Mum had put the sandwiches underneath, to keep them cool. Mum and Dad sat under the umbrella while Grandma and Grandpa played with the children.

Later Mum opened the picnic boxes and handed out sandwiches and tomatoes, crisps and cold sausages and lots of fruit. While the children had juice, the grown-ups had coffee from a thermos flask. Dad made his usual joke about real sand in the sandwiches, and Mum found little Alexander trying to put some real sand into his.

When lunch was finished, Dad stretched back and said, 'What I'd really love now is a swim.'

'So would I,' said Mum, 'but we did promise to take the children to the fair this afternoon.'

'Yes, you promised, you promised,' shouted Katie.

Grandpa looked over at Grandma, who nodded.

'Why don't we take the children to the fair?' said Grandpa, 'You know we'd love to.'

'Yes, you two could have the afternoon to yourselves,' added Grandma. 'You could have your swim. I can get the children ready for the fair.'

'That would be lovely,' said Mum.

As Grandma and Grandpa took the children back to the camp site, Grandma looked back and saw Mum and Dad running towards the sea, hand in hand. She smiled.

They all showered and changed into clean clothes, and headed down the beach road to the fairground.

'I love fairs, Grandma,' said Katie, who was so excited that she could hardly keep still.

The noise of the fair grew louder and louder as they got closer to the striped tents and painted rides. There were roundabouts with animals to ride on, a big helter skelter, dodgem cars, and all sorts of wonderful things to enjoy.

Grandpa and Katie chose to ride on the dodgem cars.

They moved smoothly round the floor, Grandpa steering them into the path of the other cars every so often. Katie screamed with delight whenever they banged into another car. It was very exciting, with the bumps, the loud music and bright lights, and the blue sparks that shot from the top of the pole on their car.

'That's where the power for the car comes from,' shouted Grandpa above the noise.

Katie just nodded. She was too excited to listen to an explanation.

Grandma and Alexander watched from the side.

Grandma took Alexander over to the roundabouts. One had just stopped, and Alexander immediately spotted a red and white car like the dodgem car that Katie and Grandpa had chosen.

'Car, car!' he shouted.

Grandma strapped him into the car and paid the fare. As the music started and the roundabout began to move, she walked around with Alexander, avoiding all the other parents, to make sure that he was safe. But when she saw how much he was enjoying the ride, she stopped and watched him go by. Behind his little red car came a small train, three horses and a fire engine, all full of laughing children. Alexander waved every time he passed Grandma, pressing the horn and shouting.

Afterwards, they all went on a little railway that took them right around the fairground. They could see the people shrieking with fear and excitement on the roller coaster, and the people who swung in their seats on the big wheel, high above the fairground.

Then they walked around and went into the hall of mirrors, where Katie was delighted to see herself as a very short and wide person, and Grandma as a very tall and thin one. She went on the ghost train next, with Grandma, and came out looking rather scared.

'But I did like it,' she said.

They stopped for fizzy drinks to cool down, and just listened to the music and watched the crowds of people moving through the fair. They could smell the hot food on the nearby stalls, and started to feel hungry. Alexander stood up and pulled at Grandma's hand.

Grandpa and Grandma took the children to see what they wanted to eat. They walked past the hot doughnut stall, past the candy floss stall and past the delicious smells of the chip van.

Grandpa bought three hot dogs, and they sat down to eat them. Alexander took his sausage out of the roll and dropped the bread. When he'd finished his sausage, he had a piece of Grandpa's.

Later on, they played the slot machines. Alexander loved pushing the coins into the slots. He was very good at it.

Grandpa had a go on the darts game, and won a gold coin and chain which he gave to Katie.

'It's beautiful, Grandpa,' she said. 'Do you think it's real gold?'

'I wouldn't be at all surprised,' said Grandpa, slipping the chain over her head.

'Fish,' said Alexander, pointing to another stall.

'So it is,' said Grandpa. 'Let's go and have a look.'

All round the stall were brightly coloured plastic fish, standing on their tails with their mouths wide open. They moved from side to side, while people put ping pong balls into their mouths. The balls rolled out of the fishes' tails and into holes at the bottom. If the balls rolled into the right hole, the player won a prize.

Grandma took out some money to buy some ping pong balls, but before she could, Alexander had taken the coins from her hand and put them into the nearest fish's mouth.

'He is silly,' said Katie. 'He thinks it's like the slot machines.'

The man in the stall looked a bit cross, but he picked up the money and gave Grandma the balls. She lifted Alexander up to put the balls into the fish's mouth. After a couple of goes, he was lucky enough to win a plastic bat and ball. Grandma helped him to unwrap his prize, but before she could stop him, he'd put the bat, ball and paper into the fish's mouth.

Of course, it all got stuck, and the man behind the stall had to stop all of the fishes to get Alexander's bat and ball out. He was beginning to look very cross.

'Thank you so much,' said Grandma, giving the man her brightest smile. 'We must be off now.'

'Good idea,' muttered the man as they left.

As they walked away, Katie was giggling behind her hand, and Grandpa was trying hard to hide a broad smile.

'I know,' he said, 'let's go and watch the fishermen bringing in their catch.'

'What's bringing in their catch, Grandpa?' asked Katie.

'It means watching them unload all the fish that they've caught,' said Grandpa.

As they got to the quayside, all the fishermen who'd hired boats for the day were returning with the fish they'd caught. Some of the fish were being sold straight away. Katie walked about, peering into the baskets and tubs of shiny fish. She bent down to look closely at one big crab which suddenly moved and made her jump backwards in surprise. As she did so, she didn't notice her necklace catch on the basket and break. The little gold coin dropped off and rolled away.

'I didn't know it was alive,' she said, as Grandpa and Alexander came up to have a look at the crab.

Alexander spotted the little gold coin, and grabbed it. Right in front of him was a young boy selling a string of six silvery mackerel that his brother had caught. Alexander immediately popped the coin into the open mouth of one of the mackerel.

'Oh, Grandpa, did you see what he just did?' cried Katie in horror. She rushed up to Alexander and gave him a shove in the chest.

'You horrible boy, that was the coin from my new gold necklace,' she shouted.

Alexander sat down with a bump, and burst into loud tears. Grandma and Grandpa rushed to pick up the two children and comfort them.

'Let's take them back to the tent,' said Grandpa to Grandma. 'I'll get us some fresh mackerel for our supper.' And he bought the six fat mackerel from the young boy.

'Don't worry, Katie,' said Grandpa, 'I'll mend your necklace when we get back, after I've cooked these fish for our tea. Perhaps you'll find your fish is a very special one.'

But Katie just sulked all the way back to the tent.

Back at the campsite, Grandpa started to prepare the fish for tea, while Alexander played outside the tent with his new bat and ball. Grandma and Katie sat out in the shade near the tent while Grandma washed the salad and the potatoes.

'Would you like to hear a story?' asked Grandma.

'What's it about?' asked Katie.

'What would you like it to be about?' asked Grandma.

'Oh, I don't care,' said Katie, who was still upset.

'Fish,' said Alexander, who had got tired of his bat and ball already.

'Very well then,' said Grandma with a smile, 'This is a story about a fish and . . . a potato!' And she held up one of the potatoes she had just cleaned.

'Oh, Grandma,' laughed Katie, 'that's silly. Whoever heard of a story about a fish and a potato!'

'If you listen,' said Grandma, 'you'll hear one.'

So Katie sat down on her camp stool and Alexander crept up to Grandma's knee.

'Now, this is the potato,' said Grandma, cutting two little eyes and a mouth into the potato she held, 'And this is the fish.' She reached into her beach bag and took out a clean sock. Putting her hand into it, she tucked the toe end between her thumb and fingers to make a mouth. Then she pushed two radishes, stalk side down, into the back of her fingers as eyes.

Katie laughed, and Alexander clapped his hands. He picked up another radish and tried to put it into the fish's mouth. Grandpa had got the mackerel ready now, and came over to sit with the others.

'They won't take more than a few minutes to cook,' he said, 'I'll just come and listen to the story as well.'

'Long, long ago,' said Grandma, putting the fish sock behind her back, 'there lived a man called Jonah.'

She walked the little potato man onto her lap.

'Now, God spoke to Jonah and said, "Go to the city of Nineveh and tell the people to stop doing wrong things or I will be very angry." But Jonah was afraid that the people of Nineveh wouldn't want him telling them what to do. So he decided to go and hide from God in another country.'

'That's silly,' said Katie, 'I know that God's not just in one country. You told me that he was everywhere.'

'That's quite true, Katie,' said Grandma, 'But Jonah wasn't as clever as you, and he thought that he could run away from God. He found a boat sailing to another country, and when the boat set sail, Jonah was fast asleep on the deck.'

Grandpa passed a small crisp lettuce leaf to Grandma and she put the potato in it, just like a little man in a boat.

'Soon,' went on Grandma, 'a great storm blew up and the boat was in danger of sinking.'

The lettuce leaf swayed around.

'The captain came up to Jonah. "We're sinking," he said. "Pray to your God to save you."

' "This is my fault," said Jonah. "Throw me overboard and the sea will be calm again. My God is angry with me, and I deserve to die." So the sailors threw Jonah overboard into the sea, because they didn't want to all be drowned.

'What happened then, Grandma?' asked Katie.

'The storm stopped, of course,' said Grandma, 'just like Jonah said it would.'

'But what happened to Jonah?' persisted Katie.

Grandma brought her hand with the fish sock on it from behind her back and opened its mouth wide.

'A huge fish came up from the depths of the sea and swallowed Jonah alive!' she said, popping the potato into the fish's mouth. Katie gasped. Grandma wrapped her hand around the potato so that it couldn't be seen.

'Jonah stayed inside the fish for three days and three nights,' said Grandma, 'and he prayed to God to save him. So God made the fish spit Jonah back out onto dry land.'

Grandma opened her hand and the sock fish dropped the potato onto Katie's lap.

'Gosh,' said Katie, 'that's amazing.'

'It certainly is,' said Grandma. 'Then God said to Jonah, "Now, do as I've told you and go and speak to the people of Nineveh. Tell them that if they don't stop doing wrong things, I shall destroy them in forty days."

'Well, Jonah knew by now that God's word must be obeyed. He had learnt his lesson, so he went to Nineveh to do God's work.'

'That's a great story,' said Katie. 'Imagine if you saw a fish spit a man up onto the beach! I think we'd better send the potato to Nineveh.'

She went and dropped the potato into the pot with the others to be cooked.

When Mum and Dad came back from the beach, they looked relaxed and happy. They'd had a lovely afternoon. Mum said it had made her feel young again, and Grandma laughed. Tea was ready; it was fish, potatoes and salad.

Katie was disappointed not to see her special potato man on her plate, but when her fish was cut open, the little potato was there, along with the gold coin.

'Look,' she said, 'it's like Jonah and the fish! Now, how did that happen?'

Grandma and Grandpa smiled at each other. Katie thought for a moment.

'Grandma, does God talk to every one?' she asked, 'I mean, even to me?'

'Why, of course,' said Grandma. 'You might not hear what he says, but you know if you are doing right or wrong, don't you? That's God talking to you.'

'Well, sometimes Mummy or Daddy has to remind me,' said Katie, 'but I know what you mean.'

Just then, Alexander reached out to Katie's plate and grabbed the potato man. Katie was about to grab it back, when she paused for a moment. Then she smiled sweetly and let him have it.

'That was very kind, Katie,' said Mum.

'I think I just got a message telling me to be kind to my baby brother,' said Katie. 'Do you think it might've been a message from God?'

'Very likely,' said Grandma.

## Poems

## The Once-a-year Fair

Each year the travelling fair comes to the common,
Caravans sparkling with cut glass and chrome,
Heavy-weight trailers stacked high with machinery,
Ready to set up their next temporary home.

Spanners and wrenches and screwdrivers flashing,
Sleeves rolled up, muscles bulge, sweat stains and oil.
Chairoplanes, roundabouts, switchbacks and dodgems,
Like mechanical flower buds, slowly uncoil.

Hot dogs and beefburgers frying with onions,
Doughnuts and candy floss, sugary-sweet,
Roll a ball! Throw a dart! Come on and try it,
But don't drip your ice cream all over my feet!

Glowing lights, flashing lights, piercing the darkness,
The night air vibrates to the pop music's sounds,
Trumpets are blaring, the diesel is roaring,
Proud painted horses go round and around.

Breathless and queasy, with pockets quite empty,
Bruised from our rides in the squat dodgem cars,
Homebound, we stop to look back at the fairground
That shines in the night like a spaceship from Mars.

The common was empty the next time I saw it,
With hardly a sign of the travellers there;
Marks in the grass and a trampled, torn poster
Were all that remained of the once-a-year fair.

## The late arrivals

As we bump across the dunes,
Headlights bright as harvest moons,
Sallow moths rise from the gorse
And float around a grazing horse.
Past the tangled mounds of bramble,
Where the marram-grass roots ramble,
Lanterns shine on tired faces,
Blue camp-beds and unpacked cases.
'We'll help you raise your tent,' they said,
'Or else you'll never get to bed.'
Metal tent poles slide and clatter,
Tired children yawn and chatter;
While the canvas cover's shaken,
Other curious children waken.
Pegs are hammered, guy ropes stretched,
Beds inflated, water fetched.
Though the dawn is close at hand,
Happy children dig the sand,
Lit by headlights from the cars
And the ever-fading stars.
A grey light creeps across the hill
And everyone is very still;
Munching biscuits, sipping tea,
Listening to the whispering sea.
A lark leaps to the rising sun;
Another holiday begun.

## Reading

*From Psalm 107: 23–29*

They that go down to the sea in ships,
That do business in great waters;
These people see the works of the Lord,
And his wonders in the deep.

For he commands, and raises the stormy wind,
Which lifts up the waves of the sea.
They mount up to heaven, they go down again to the depths:
Their soul is melted because of trouble.
They reel to and fro, and stagger like a drunken man,
And are at their wits' end.

Then they cry to the Lord in their trouble,
And he brings them out of their distress.
He makes the storm a calm,
So that the waves are still.

## Prayers

For the sea that we enjoy on our holidays,
For the fish that swim in the sea,
For all the sailors who work in ships,
We thank you, Lord.
Amen.

We know you love us, Lord.
Help us to listen to your words,
And to obey your commandments.
Wherever we are, you are always with us.
Amen.

## End of the Assembly

## Follow-up classwork

Make a hand puppet from an old sock. Give it eyes, ears, nose and hair.

With some friends, make up a play for your puppets.

Make a fairground with all the rides.

Write a poem about fairs.

Find out as much as you can about whales and dolphins. Which organisations protect whales? Write a letter to one for some information on what they do.

## Further reading

**Jonah and the Great Fish** B. Hollyer (Macdonald)
**Michael and the Sea** A. Coles (Hodder & Stoughton)
**At the Fair** L. Ivory (Burke Books)
**Beach Boy** N. Smee (Collins)
**Joe At the Fair** D. Roberts (Oxford University Press)
**Thank you, God, for our Day at the Beach** E. Reeves (Scripture Union)

**ASSEMBLY 15**

# Mum's birthday cake

## The prodigal son

*Luke 15:11–32 (See also vs. 3–7 and 8–10)*

---

This Assembly deals with the story of the prodigal son. (Other parables on the same theme are The Lost Coin and The Lost Sheep.) The parable tells us of the joy God has in the sinner who repents. This theme can be introduced to children with reference to these parables, and to the story 'Mum's Birthday Cake.'

Further themes that can be discussed are:
How to cope with feelings of jealousy.
How important the thought behind the gift is.

## Songs and hymns

**And God said The Sun Should Shine** (*3*) Come and Sing (*Scripture Union*)
**Supermum** (*24*) Tinderbox (*Black*)
**The Flowers that Grow In the Garden** (*53*) Someone's Singing, Lord (*Black*)

## Read the story

## Mum's birthday cake

It was the morning before Mum's birthday, and the weather was beautiful. Alexander was playing happily in the sand pit, while Cosmo the cat slept under a nearby hedge. Mum and Katie were busy at the top of the garden cutting flowers.

'Will these go all brown and die soon, like the roses we picked?' asked Katie.

'No, not these,' said Mum. 'These are special flowers. They'll keep their shape and colour right through until next spring.'

They carried the big basket of flowers into the house, where Mum cut the stems off, and laid the flowers head-down on a tray to dry out. Katie watched her carefully.

'Why have you cut off most of the stalk?' she asked. 'You always tell me to leave a long stalk when I pick flowers.'

'I want these flowers to dry out now,' explained Mum. 'If I leave too much stalk it may shrivel up. I shall thread a piece of wire into the little bit of stalk that's left, and use that to arrange them.'

'They don't have a smell,' said Katie, bending right down to sniff at them. 'And they're all prickly and stiff like . . . like . . .'

'Like straw,' said Mum with a laugh. 'They're called straw flowers, you know.'

'You picked ever so many,' said Katie. 'Are you going to do a flower arrangement?' She held up some of the flower heads to admire the colours, which ranged from golds and browns to pinks and lilacs. She quickly put one as pink as strawberry ice cream to her tongue, but of course, there was no taste, either.

'Yes, I shall be doing a very special arrangement with these,' said Mum. 'I'm making a Harvest Cross for St. Mary's Church, for the Harvest Festival in a few weeks. Because it will be made with straw flowers, the cross will last all winter, as well, and brighten up some dark corner of the church. That'll be nice, won't it?'

'Oh, yes,' said Katie. She was silent for a while, then, all in a rush, she said, 'I've got a secret to tell you. I've been making something, as well. I made your birthday card last night, when you went swimming. Daddy helped me. Alex did one too, but it's not as good as mine.'

'Well, don't tell me any more, or it won't be much of a secret, will it?' said Mum, then she suddenly shouted, 'Stop right where you are!'

Katie was surprised.

'I wasn't going to tell you any more,' she started, then realised that her mum hadn't been talking to her.

'No, not you, darling,' laughed Mum. 'Him!'

She pointed at Alexander, who had come to the back door, completely covered in sand. He stopped in surprise, and sand fell off his hair and clothes into a heap around him. Mum went and started to brush off the worst of it.

'I won't ask how you did this,' she said, shaking sand out of his thick brown hair, 'but I think you need a bath right away!'

She carried Alexander upstairs, and in a few minutes, Katie could hear the bath running. She started happily sorting the flowers into different colours until Mum came back downstairs with all of Alexander's clothes. She threw the armful into the washing machine.

'He'll be quite happy for a while,' said Mum. 'At least, until he's emptied the bath water all over the floor. I'll just do this washing, and get it out to dry before I start on the Harvest Cross.'

'When are you going to make your birthday cake, then?' asked Katie.

Mum just laughed.

'Oh, I'm far too old for a birthday cake, darling,' she said with a laugh. 'Besides, I'm going to be too busy with the Harvest Cross to find time for cake-making.'

'But that's not fair,' complained Katie. 'You made Dad a cake for *his* birthday.'

Katie felt sad that Mum wouldn't have a birthday cake. She thought how awful it would be if her own birthday came and nobody had made her a cake. She tried to be as helpful as she could, so that Mum shouldn't feel sad about her cake. She tidied up Alexander's bath toys when he finally came out of the bath, and helped her mum find his clean clothes when she was dressing him. She even managed to keep him out of the sand pit for a short time when he was allowed outside to play again. But she was still feeling a bit sad when Grandma phoned after lunch and asked if Katie would like to come to her house for a while.

'Oh, yes, please,' said Katie.

By the time Grandma came to collect Katie, Alexander was next door, playing in the back garden with Brenda, the lady who lived there. Grandma waved to Brenda, whose cheeks were getting rather pink as she ran up and down the path with Alexander chasing happily after.

'It's a bit hot for that sort of game,' said Grandma to Mum, as they went into the kitchen.

'I think they both enjoy it,' said Mum. 'Well, I know Alex does! I'm sure Brenda will send him back when she's had enough.'

Katie ran up to give Grandma a kiss.

'What are you two going to get up to this afternoon, then?' asked Mum.

'Oh, this and that,' said Grandma.

Katie ran down the front path to Grandma's car, and Grandma strapped her into the back seat. As they drove off to

Grandma's house, Katie asked, 'What does "this and that" mean, Grandma?'

'Well, in this case, it means that you're going to make your mum a birthday cake,' answered Grandma.

'Oh, that's great,' said Katie, delighted. 'You know, I've been feeling sad all day because I thought that Mum wasn't going to have a cake. But I don't really know how to make a proper cake. I've only made pretend ones before.'

'That's all right,' said Grandma, 'I'll be there to help you.'

In the kitchen, Grandma put an apron round Katie's waist and turned on the oven. Katie got the margarine and eggs out of the fridge, while Grandma took the flour and sugar down from the cupboard. Grandma took down the big weighing scales from a high shelf, and Katie weighed out all of the ingredients.

'This is quite hard work,' said Katie, as she beat the sugar and margarine with a wooden spoon.

'Why don't you rub some margarine round the cake tin, while I finish beating that,' suggested Grandma. 'It's almost ready now, anyway.'

Then Grandma showed Katie how to add the beaten eggs and flour to the mixture, and finally, they added a drop of milk.

'That's just to get the right consistency,' said Grandma.

'What's a consistency?' asked Katie.

'Well, it means it's wet enough to drop off the wooden spoon, but not so sloppy that it would just run off the spoon,' said Grandma. They carefully spooned the cake mixture into the big cake tin, then they filled some small paper cases with what was left over. Soon all the cakes were in the oven, and Grandma and Katie cleaned up and washed their hands.

'That was fun,' said Katie. 'But it was quite difficult. I'm glad you helped me.'

'It was my pleasure,' laughed Grandma, as she got them both a glass of lemonade. They went and sat in the garden and sipped their drinks.

'Can we put some icing on next?' asked Katie.

'We'll have to wait for it to cool down after it comes out of the oven,' said Grandma. 'And I have a special treat for your mum. Instead of ordinary icing, we're going to cover the cake in marshmallows. I haven't made her a cake like that since she was a little girl. She used to love marshmallow topping.'

Later, when the cake was cool enough, Grandma got out the

packet of pink and white marshmallows. Katie pushed at one with her finger. It was soft and squashy. The dent her finger had made slowly disappeared.

'I think you'd better eat that one you've been poking around,' said Grandma. 'Then you can spread some jam on top of the cake. That will help the marshmallows to stick to it.'

Once the cake was spread with jam, Grandma put lots of marshmallows close together on top. Then she put the cake under the hot grill. In a short time, the marshmallows were beautifully toasted and the cake was ready.

When they got back home, Katie couldn't wait to show the cake to her mum. She dashed into the house, calling, 'Mum! Mum! Come and see! There's a surprise!'

'Whatever is it?' asked Mum. 'What's the surprise? Who's it for?'

'For you, of course,' said Katie. 'Look, here's Grandma, carrying it in a box.'

Mum opened the lid of the box and looked inside.

'Oh, what a lovely cake,' she said. 'And it's even got toasted marshmallows on top! Did Grandma make it?'

'No, it was me,' said Katie, excitedly, then she added, 'Grandma did help me, though.'

'Well, perhaps we can start my birthday today,' said Mum. 'Shall we have a slice of cake with our cup of tea?'

'Oh, no, you don't,' smiled Grandma. 'Katie made some little cakes as well. You can leave cutting your cake until tomorrow.'

They decided to take their cakes and tea out into the garden, and sat near the back door.

Alexander was out in the garden, and they could see him busy with his little spade in the sand pit and the water bucket. After a while, he came up carrying an old tin plate. On the plate was a grubby mixture of wet soil and sand, and poked into the mixture were some of Mum's straw flowers, some dandelions and a few leaves. He handed the plate to his mum with a big smile.

'What's this, then?' she asked.

'Birthday cake,' said Alexander.

'Why, it's lovely,' said Mum. 'It's a really beautiful cake.'

She was obviously delighted, and Katie noticed that she didn't seem to mind at all that Alex was scattering sand everywhere, and had become just as dirty as he had been before his bath. She picked him up and kissed and cuddled him.

'But Mum, he's used your special flowers, and they've got all covered in mud,' complained Katie.

'That's all right,' said Mum, and kissed Alexander again. 'Now I've got two wonderful birthday cakes. I'm very lucky.'

Katie said nothing and went up to her room. A little while later, Grandma came in.

'Is anything the matter?' she asked.

Katie was sitting on her bed, looking out of the window. She shook her head, and Grandma could see the shine of a tear on her cheek.

'Mum liked Alex's cake better than mine,' she said in a small sad voice.

'I'm sure that's not true,' said Grandma, sitting on the bed next to Katie.

'Yes, it is,' said Katie. 'She cuddled him and made a big fuss of him. She didn't do that to me. She thinks that it's more important when he does something for her.'

'Does that make you feel jealous?' asked Grandma, but Katie just shook her head again, and carried on looking out of the window.

'Let me see,' said Grandma. 'That reminds me of something that happened a long time ago. Shall I tell you about it?'

Katie didn't answer her, but just carried on looking out of the window. As Grandma carried on talking, Katie leaned back against her.

'This is a story that Jesus told,' said Grandma. 'A long time ago there lived a man who had two sons. One day, the younger son came to him and asked him for the share of money that would be his when his father died. His father gave him the money, and the younger son went away to another country. He had soon wasted all the money, and had to get a job looking after pigs to keep himself alive.

'One day he thought to himself that even his father's servants had plenty of food, while he was hungry. So he decided to go home.

'When his father saw him coming home, he ran out to meet him.

'The son said, "Father, I've sinned against you and against heaven. I don't deserve to be your son any more, but I would like to be one of your servants."

'But the father was so pleased to have his son home again that he gave him lots of new clothes and presents, and made a big fuss of him. He gave a big feast to celebrate his son's return. He told all of his friends, "My son was lost, but now he's been found again."

'But when the man's older son heard about all of the fuss his father was making about the younger son's return, he was very jealous. He said to his father, "I've worked hard for you all these years, and never disobeyed you, but you never made a big fuss of me, or gave me presents like you have given my brother."

'His father said, "My son, you've always stayed with me, and everything I have is yours. But your brother had left us, and now he's come back. It was as though he had died, and now he's alive again. No wonder I want to celebrate.'

Katie was still looking out the window, and when Grandma finished the story, she sighed.

'Do you know what Jesus was telling us in that story?' asked Grandma.

'Is it not to be jealous of our brothers?' asked Katie.

'Not really,' answered Grandma. 'You see, sometimes we take people for granted if they're always with us. And we sometimes take for granted the things that people can do. Now, your mummy knows what a clever girl you are, so she wasn't really surprised that you made her a cake, although she was very pleased. But when she saw that Alex had made her a cake as well, it was a complete surprise. You know he can be a bit naughty sometimes, and I think she kissed him because she was so pleased that he was being so good and kind to her. The father in the story loved both of his sons the same, but when the one he thought was gone for ever came back to him, he was ever so happy, and wanted to celebrate. Do you see?'

'Yes,' said Katie. 'And I can see something else, as well. Cosmo is eating Alex's cake.'

Grandma jumped up and looked out of the window. Sure enough, there was Cosmo the cat licking between the straw flowers on Alexander's cake. Grandma and Katie ran downstairs.

When Mum saw what Cosmo was doing, she laughed. She picked up the cake and sniffed at it.

'Oh, no, he's mixed cat food in with the sand and dirt,' she laughed. 'I hope your cake hasn't got any cat food in, Katie.'

'No,' said Grandma. 'There's no cat food in Katie's cake. Just a dead mouse or two.'

'Yuck,' said Katie.

# Poems

## The loving cake

I will make you a seaside cake.
Water for the sand when the tide comes in,
Stirred and mixed in a bucket of tin,
Smoothed and patted, turned upside down,
Shell decorated and seaweed crowned.
Foam cream topping from the ebb-tide's wake,
Served in the middle of a salt water lake.

I will make you a garden cake.
Soil and sand, green water from the pond,
Duckweed, watercress and slime to bond,
Stirred with a stick in a red flower pot,
Iced with a daisy chain tied in a knot.
Left for an hour for the sun to bake,
Careful how you cut it, the pot might break.

I will make you a loving cake,
Of paper and cardboard and bright decorations,
Filled with happiness, never vexations.
I'll wash up, I'll dry up, I'll tidy the house,
Not shout or get angry, I won't even grouse.
Mix all the fine promises I want to make
And give them to you in my sweet loving cake.

## Helichrysum

Helichrysum, flower of straw,
Lovely and without a flaw.
Strong and sturdy, standing proud
Amid the sundrenched garden crowd.

Petals with a glossy shine,
Gleam in shades of ruby wine,
Citrus yellow, pearly white,
Amethyst and copper bright.

Insects crowd around your head,
From your pollen bees are fed;

Yet you lend no sweet perfume
To scent the darkened evening room.

But your stiff and straw-dry head
Stays with us when summer's dead,
Reminds us in the cold December
Of the summer's golden splendour.

And, while winter's snows are passing,
Your sweet face is everlasting.
Picked one summer's shining hour,
Helichrysum, timeless flower.

## Reading

### *Luke 15:8–10*

'Or suppose a woman who has ten silver coins loses one of them – what does she do?
She lights a lamp, sweeps her house, and looks carefully everywhere until she finds it.
When she finds it, she calls her friends and neighbours together, and says to them,
'I am so happy I found the coin I lost. Let us celebrate!'
In the same way, I tell you, the angels of God rejoice over one sinner who repents.'

## Prayers

To God, who gives our daily bread
A thankful song we raise,
And pray that he who sends us food
May fill our hearts with praise.

*T. Tallis 1510–1585*

There are times, God, when I feel a badness inside me,
It makes me forget all the wonderful things I have;
It makes me hate people.
The name of this badness is jealousy.
I envy others for the things they have,
Or for the people they are.
Please help me to overcome this terrible feeling
So that I can understand that all I really need is your love.
Amen.

## End of the Assembly

## Follow-up classwork

Bake a cake. Use: 8 oz. margarine, 8 oz. sugar, 10 oz. flour, 4 eggs and a little milk. Use the creaming method to make one large or several small cakes.

When the cake is cool, spread the top with jam, arrange marshmallows on the top and toast them under a grill.

Make a big cardboard 'loving cake'. Discuss with the children some simple ways to show love for their friends (E.g. I will lend my crayons, I will give up my turn at the sand pit etc.) Write them down and place these 'promises' into the cake. Each person can then pull out a promise in turn.

Late Summer activities:

Collect grasses and dry them for winter displays.

Press flowers for Christmas calendars.

If available, pick and store straw flowers for winter display.

Plant bulbs for winter flowering.

## Further reading

**The Cake That Mack Ate** R. Robart & K. M. Kowalski (Viking Kestrel)

**The Cake Maker** A. Braithwaite (Dinosaur)

**The Magic Birthday Cake** S. May (Deutsch)

**A Secret for Grandma's Birthday** F. Brandenberg (Hamish Hamilton)

ASSEMBLY 16

# It's mine!

## (The judgement of Solomon)
*1 Kings 3:16–28*

---

This Assembly introduces the story of the judgement of Solomon. It is hoped that the following themes can be discussed in classwork:

Helping to sort out other people's problems.
Being fair.
Telling the truth.
Listening and learning.
Taking care of library books (and things in general).

## Songs and hymns

**Lost and Found** (*57*) Come and Praise (*BBC*)
**It's Me, O Lord** (*51*) Alleluya (*Black*)
**Jesus' Hands Were Kind Hands** (*33*) Someone's Singing, Lord (*Black*)
**The Sun That Shines Across The Sea** (*11*) Someone's Singing, Lord

## Read the Story

## It's mine!

'It's mine!' screamed Jenny, clutching the little blue train.

Alexander tried to grab the train, but Jenny pushed him away with her free hand. In frustration, Alexander smacked the little girl hard, but that only made her scream even louder.

'It's mine!'

Alexander started to howl with rage and Katie came into the room to see what they were up to.

'It's mine, Katie,' said Jenny, who was beginning to cry.

'No, mine!' shouted Alexander, making another grab for the train.

'Actually,' said Katie, 'this is my train.' She prised it away from Jenny's little fingers. Now both children set up such a wail that Cosmo the cat ran out of the room and Katie's mum came in.

'What on earth's going on here?' asked Mum.

'It's them,' said Katie. 'They're at it again. They're fighting over this blue train engine, so I've taken it away from them both. But they're still making a fuss.'

'Well of course they are,' said Mum. 'Don't you think it would be a better idea if you gave them both a train to play with?'

She handed a red engine to Alexander and a green one to Jenny. Alexander immediately threw his engine to the ground and held up his arms to his mum for a cuddle. Jenny stopped crying, grabbed both engines and rushed off into the other room. Mum sighed and picked Alexander up. He stopped crying straight away, and gave her a big smile.

'What a lot of noise about nothing,' said Mum.

'It certainly is,' said Katie. 'I do wish I could stop them fighting over everything.'

'I think that would be easier said than done,' smiled Mum. 'Look, why don't you go and see if Jenny's all right, while I give Alex some warm milk. I think he may be getting a bit tired.'

Katie found Jenny sitting in a corner by the toy cupboard looking very fierce. She brightened up, though, when she saw that it was Katie, not Alexander, who had come to find her.

'Shall we go up to my room and play with my ponies?' Katie asked.

'Oh, yes, please,' said Jenny, and the two girls went upstairs to Katie's room.

After Alexander had finished his warm milk, Mum took him up to his room for a nap. When he had fallen asleep, she popped her head round Katie's door.

'What good girls you are, playing so nicely together,' she said. 'Now, make sure you don't wake Alex up, won't you?'

'We won't,' said Katie. They played quietly and happily together until Alexander woke up refreshed from his nap.

The girls heard him singing and talking to himself in his room, so they went in to see him. He was waving a small brown bear around in the air and saying, 'Here's Super Ted, flying through the air.'

'Can we play with you?' asked Katie.

Alexander nodded happily, and the two girls picked up a soft toy each and made them fly around with Super Ted. Of course, in a few minutes, Alexander decided that he wanted to fly the white bear that Jenny was playing with. He politely offered her his brown bear, then grabbed the white one and started to pull.

'It's mine!' shrieked Jenny, and the fight started all over again.

'Stop it, stop it!' shouted Katie. 'Listen, I think that's Mum calling us for dinner. Let's go downstairs.'

Of course, Katie hadn't really heard her mum calling, she just wanted to stop the little ones fighting. It was still a little while before dinner, so Katie decided to try and teach Jenny and Alexander to share toys nicely. She took them to the toy cupboard and made them sit down on the floor in front of it.

'Now,' said Katie, trying to sound like Mum. 'Let's play with some toys. Jenny, you choose a toy.'

Jenny chose a rabbit, and hugged it to her chest, with a glare at Alexander. He chose the little blue train that had caused all the trouble earlier on.

'That's my train,' said Jenny, immediately, still holding the rabbit but trying to get the train from Alexander.

'No it's not, Jenny,' said Katie. 'I know you've got one like it at home, but this one's mine. I've had it for ages and I let Alex share it with me. Now, wouldn't you like to let him have it while you have the rabbit?'

'No!' shouted Jenny, dropping the rabbit to reach for the train.

Katie realised that her plan wasn't going to work. She decided to try something else.

'Come with me, you two,' she said, and led them to the settee.

'Now, you sit at one end, Jenny, and Alexander can sit at the other end. That way, you can't grab each other's toys. Now, I'll go and get a big pile of toys for each of you.'

It took quite a while to bring two piles of toys from the cupboard, with having to keep putting Alexander back on the settee every time he got off, but eventually Katie stood back to survey the loaded settee.

'There you are,' she said. 'Now you've got all the toys you could possibly want.'

Of course, you can guess what happened. After only a few minutes, the little children were fighting over the same picture book.

'It's mine!' shouted Jenny, pulling at the book.

'No, it's mine!' shouted Alexander, pulling just as hard.

'Stop it, stop it!' shouted Katie. 'You'll tear the book in half.'

But as soon as she had said those words, she had an idea. She remembered a story that her teacher, Mrs Maine, had told them a few days before. She ran upstairs, while the other two were still fighting over the book, and came back with her special cutting out scissors.

Taking the book from the children, she carefully cut it in half, along the fabric binding. It was quite difficult, and took her a little while, but the other two watched her in horrified fascination, without a word.

'How about that, then?' she asked, handing each of them a half of the book. 'Now you can both have the book!'

Jenny and Alexander looked at the halves of the book, and at each other. They both began to cry. Alexander threw his half of the book down and ran to find his mum. Jenny picked up both halves and followed him.

Katie was amazed. What ever could you do with children like that? It seemed that nothing could please them. She shrugged, and began to tidy up all the toys from the settee.

Out in the kitchen, Grandma and Auntie Susan had just come back from their shopping trip, and were having a cup of tea with Mum, when the two howling children rushed in. Jenny was still holding the two halves of the picture book, and ran straight to Auntie Susan to show her.

'Oh, Jenny, did you do that?' asked Auntie Susan in dismay. But little Jenny just cried louder and shook her head.

Just then, Katie came in.

'Katie, do you know about this?' asked Mum.

'Oh, yes, I did that,' said Katie, beginning to realise that it hadn't been such a good idea after all.

'That's a terrible thing to do to a book,' said Mum. 'But it's even worse to do it to a library book!'

'Oh, Mum, I didn't know it was a library book!' said Katie, horrified.

Mum opened the front of the book to show Katie the page with all the dates stamped on, and the cardboard pocket for the ticket.

Katie felt awful. What would they say at the library? Would they ever let her borrow another book? Tears began to run down her cheeks.

Grandma took the halves of the book from Mum and looked

at the cover. She gave a small smile, and whispered to Mum. Then she turned to Katie.

'Why did you cut the book in half, Katie?' she asked. 'It's not like you to be naughty.'

'It was to stop them fighting,' said Katie tearfully. 'I'd tried everything else, and they were still fighting over the same toy all the time. Then, when they were both pulling at the book, I remembered a story that Mrs Maine told us.'

'Oh, good,' said Grandma. 'A story. I do hope you're going to tell it to us. Let's all go and sit down in the front room.'

Mum took Alexander and Auntie Susan carried Jenny, and they all settled down in the front room for Katie's story.

'All right, then,' said Katie, blowing her nose on a tissue. 'Are you all ready?'

'Yes, please,' said her mum, so Katie began.

'Once upon a time, before Jesus was born, there was a king called King Solomon. He was a very clever man. One day two women went to see him. One of them was carrying a baby. The other woman said, "That's my baby. Last night, her baby died, so she stole mine and said it was hers. But it's mine."

' "No, it's not," said the woman who was holding the baby. "It's mine!"

'So King Solomon thought, then he said, "All right, then. I'll cut the baby in half with a sword and you can have half each." '

Katie paused.

'Well, that's how I got the idea about cutting the book in half,' she explained. 'I thought that if a clever man like King Solomon did it, it must be a good idea.'

'But what happened next?' asked Grandma. 'In the story, I mean. We know what happened here.'

'I don't really know,' admitted Katie. 'I didn't listen to the rest of the story. I was thinking about Alexander being cut in half.'

'Would that be a good thing?' asked Mum with a smile.

'Oh, no, Mummy!' said Katie. 'I know he's a bit naughty, and I do get cross with him sometimes, but I really do love him.'

'Well, that's how the real mother got her baby back,' said Grandma. 'Because she loved him. When King Solomon offered to have the baby cut in half, she said, "Oh, please don't cut him in half. Let her keep him, but don't kill him."

'But the other woman said, "I don't care if you cut him in half; at least she won't have a baby either."

'King Solomon knew that the first woman was the real mother, and gave her the baby.'

'I'm glad you told me the rest of the story, Grandma,' said Katie. 'I wondered what happened.'

'It's a pity you didn't listen in the first place,' said Mum. 'Then you might not have cut a library book in half.'

'Well, I might just be able to do something about that,' said Grandma with a smile at Mum.

She put both pieces of the book into her large handbag, and shook it up and down. Then she put in her hand and pulled out the book, all shiny and new, and in one piece.

'How on earth did you do that, Grandma?' asked Katie, very impressed. 'And don't say magic, because I know it wasn't.'

'All right,' said Grandma with a laugh. 'I'll tell you. You were talking about this book a week or so ago, and when I saw it at the shops today, I decided to buy it for you as a special present. Of course, I didn't know that you'd already borrowed it from the library.'

'I'm very glad you did buy it,' said Mum. 'Now we can take the new book to the library to replace the one that was cut in half. I'm sure that they'll be happy to exchange them. I'll mend the cut one for you, Katie, so that you'll have something to remind you never to damage a book again. You should treat books with respect, you know.'

'Yes, and I really am sorry,' said Katie. 'It just seemed like the only way to stop them fighting. But it didn't work. I don't suppose I'm as wise as King Solomon.'

After dinner, Auntie Susan inflated some balloons for the children to play with. Of course, Jenny and Alexander both wanted the same one, but when they started to fight over it, it burst with a loud bang, scaring them both. After that, they were both quite good, and neither of them said 'It's mine' for the rest of the afternoon.

## Poems

## The dandelion is mine

You can have sweet roses
And the honeysuckle vine,

Petunia and forget-me-not,
But the dandelion is mine.

You can have the forest,
With its beech and oak and pine,
And shady ferns and bluebells,
But the dandelion is mine.

You can have the golden beach,
The sea wind fresh with brine,
Sea pinks and yellow samphire,
But the dandelion is mine.

The dandelion is all I want;
Sweet tousled head of gold,
Worshipping the summer sun
Until its mane is grey and old.

## Grandpa

My Grandpa, who is very wise,
Can tell the truth from people's eyes.
He knows just when they tell a lie,
And never needs to ask them why.

He says that he can read your mind,
And knows just who is true or kind.
Most robbers wouldn't stand a chance;
He'd stop them with a knowing glance.

And yet I think it very strange
That he forgets some people's names.
He calls them 'Pal' or 'Mate' or 'Chum,'
He'll smile and talk to anyone.

When we play games, he never wins,
He says, 'Well done,' and then he grins.
How can a man, who is so wise,
Not score at football, though he tries?

Through all the years he's watched me grow,
My Grandpa's taught me all I know;

Some day I hope that I will be
As wise and gentle, kind as he.

## Reading

## Solomon's judgement

### *1 Kings 3:23–28*

Then King Solomon said,
'Each of you claims that the living child is hers and that the dead child belongs to the other one.'
He sent for a sword, and when it was brought, he said,
'Cut the living child in two and give each woman half of it.'
The real mother, her heart full of love for her son, said to the king,
'Please, Your Majesty, don't kill the child! Give it to her!'
But the other woman said,
'Don't give it to either of us; go ahead and cut it in two.'
Then Solomon said,
'Don't kill the child! Give it to the first woman – she is its real mother.'

When the people of Israel heard of Solomon's decision, they were all filled with deep respect for him, because they knew then that God had given him the wisdom to settle disputes fairly.

## Prayers

Dear God,
Sometimes we are accused of doing wrong
When we are innocent.
Sometimes no one will believe what we say.
You know what is true and what is right.
Help us always to put our trust in you.
Amen.

Thank you, God, for our library books,
Books for scientists, books for cooks,
Books for someone who loves to read,
Books of adventure and noble deeds,
Books of poetry, books of fun,
The Bible to read when work is done.

Brand new or dog-eared, whatever their looks,
Thank you, God, for our library books.
Amen.

## End of the Assembly

## Follow-up classwork

Sharing

Make small salt and flour cakes and tarts for a party. How many cakes altogether? Shared equally between toys, how many each?

Make collections of buttons, yogurt cartons, washers, bottle tops, counters, unifix etc. With the children in groups, share the items equally between children. How many altogether? How many each? (Sharing between two children, half the total each, sharing between four children, a quarter of the total each, etc. – introduction to fractions.)

Make your collection of books into a library. Sort into groups of information and story books. Sort them, and say how many ways you can sort them. Look at some old books. (Ask parents and grandparents for copies.)

Make paper books, print using blocks, scrap material and potatoes.

## Further reading

**Bet you Can't** P. Dale (Walker Books)
**I am Better Than You** R. Lopshire (World's Work)
**Everybody Said No** S. Larelle (Black)

**ASSEMBLY 17**

# And the walls came tumbling down

(The fall of Jericho)
*Joshua 5: 13–15 and 6: 1–27*

---

This Assembly introduces the story of Joshua bringing down the walls of Jericho. It shows us that God uses silence and noise to achieve his purpose. 'O clap your hands, all ye people: shout unto God with the voice of triumph. For the Lord most high . . . is a great King over all the Earth.' (Psalm 47:1–2) 'Be still, and know that I am God.' (Psalm 46:10)

Other themes which can be discussed with the children are:

What happens when people get over-excited.
The pleasures of anticipation.

## Songs and hymns

**If You're Happy And You Know It** (*79*) Flying a Round (*Black*)
**Tra La That a'way** (*p15*) Ten Galloping Horses (*Warne*)
**Joshua Fit the Battle of Jericho** (*70*) Alleluya (*Black*)

## Read the story

## And the walls came tumbling down

One Saturday morning, Katie woke up very early, just as it was getting light. She crept out of bed and over to the window where she looked out at the frosty autumn garden in the dawn light. The apple tree had lost all of its leaves, but there were still a few bright red apples hanging on the branches, like forgotten Christmas tree ornaments. She shivered. It was cold. Even the donkey, standing silently in his field at the end of the garden, was wearing a woollen jacket, and a cobweb in the corner of the window was white with frost and frozen dewdrops.

What could have woken her up so early? Suddenly the bedroom door burst open, and her little brother Alexander rushed into the room.

'It's Bonfire Night!' he shrieked, waving his arms around like a mad Catherine wheel. 'Whizz, bang, bang, whoosh!'

'It's only Bonfire Morning at the moment,' said Katie, sternly, 'and there won't be any bonfire or fireworks until tonight.'

But Alexander kept dashing around the room being a firework, and making firework noises.

'You're going to give me a headache,' shouted Katie, with her hands over her ears.

Mum came into the room just then, and picked Alexander up.

'Back to bed,' she said. 'I'm sorry, Katie, but he's got himself all worked up about tonight. They've been talking about Bonfire Night at his playgroup, and he and Jenny are very excited about it. They did a dance where they pretended to be fireworks, and I think he's still doing it.'

Mum was right. Alexander carried on dashing about and doing his firework dance, accompanied by firework noises. Later on, Auntie Susan phoned up and said that little Jenny was very excited, and being rather silly. Mum told her that Alex was just as bad.

'I think it might be a good idea to take them both out for a long walk,' said Auntie Susan. 'Perhaps we can tire them out so that they'll have a good nap before this evening, and be a bit calmer for the display.'

Mum agreed, and they arranged to meet at the field where the firework display was due to be held that evening. After an early lunch, they set off.

Although the sun was bright, the grass that was in the shade was still white and crunchy with frost. Katie walked carefully through it, looking behind her at the trail of footprints she had left. They met Auntie Susan and Jenny at the field. Jenny and Alexander dashed about the field in their wellington boots, shouting at the tops of their voices. They shouted at the huge bonfire that was still being built, and dashed back and forth under the rope that was to keep the crowds well back from the fire.

At the far side of the field was a fair. It came every year to the same spot, and Katie could remember it from the year before.

'I had a ride on the roundabout last year,' she said.

This set Jenny and Alexander off on a new course. They both wanted to go on the roundabout, they wanted hot dogs and ice creams, and they wanted fireworks, all at once.

'No,' said Mum and Auntie Susan together.

'That will all happen tonight,' explained Auntie Susan. 'You must wait just a little longer for your treats.'

But nothing could make the little children unhappy. They dashed about and shouted as much as before. Katie felt worn out.

When they all got back to Katie's house, Mum switched on the television, hoping to take their minds off Bonfire Night, but the first thing they saw was a firework display, then a programme about Guy Fawkes. Jenny and Alexander shouted and danced all the way through it.

'They don't look very tired yet, Mummy,' said Katie.

Grandma came round in her car, and said that she was going shopping.

'Would anyone like to come with me?' she asked.

'Me, please,' said Katie straight away, 'Then I can get a bit of peace away from those two.'

'Well, we could all do with a bit of peace away from these two,' smiled Auntie Susan. 'They've been like this since play-group last Thursday, and now it's Saturday. None of us has had a proper night's sleep for ages. But I think we'd better stay here and try to get them to have a nap.'

'All right, then, we'll see you later,' said Grandma. 'I'll tell you what, I'll give Katie her tea, and bring her home in time for the firework display this evening.'

She and Katie set off to the big supermarket nearby and afterwards, they went back to Grandma's house for tea.

When Grandpa came home from work, Grandma and Katie were fast asleep in the dark, with the television on and their empty tea cups and plates beside them. He laughed, and the sudden noise woke them up.

'That was a nice sleep,' said Katie, stretching.

'Well, at least we'll be rested for tonight,' said Grandma.

'Oh, yes,' said Grandpa. 'What time's the big firework display?'

'We'll go as soon as you've had your tea,' said Grandma, 'The fireworks start at 7.30.'

After Grandpa had had his tea, he and Grandma dressed in lots of warm clothes, and took Katie back home to get changed.

Alexander and Jenny still hadn't had a nap. They had

shouted and done their firework dance all afternoon, and Mum and Auntie Susan were looking worn out. Katie's dad had got quite cross at teatime, when they had sausages for tea. He'd said, 'Oh, good, bangers for tea,' and the two little ones had giggled and shoved each other every time they put a fork into a sausage.

They were all glad when Uncle Paul, Jenny's dad, arrived, and it was time to get ready to go. Mum and Auntie Susan wrapped the two little ones up warmly, in scarves, hats and wellington boots, with mittens safely threaded through their sleeves.

'Are we taking pushchairs?' asked Katie's dad.

'No, not pushchairs,' said Jenny.

'Not pushchairs,' agreed Alexander.

The family all set off through the rising mist to the field where the bonfire would soon be lit. All the way along the lanes, two pairs of wellington boots splashed in every puddle, and two excited little voices shouted about fireworks and fairgrounds.

When they reached the field, the fairground was in full swing at one side, while people streamed towards the bonfire on the other side. There was a delicious smell of hot dogs and chips on the air, and in the distance an occasional rocket lit the night sky. They went to the edge of the rope near the bonfire where they could all get a good view of the display. Jenny and Alexander sat on their daddies' shoulders.

Soon the bonfire was lit, and hot tongues of flames warmed their faces. The first of the fireworks zoomed into the sky, exploding like coloured flowers. Everybody said 'Oohh' and 'Aahh'.

'I don't believe this,' said Dad, 'Alexander's fallen asleep.'

'So has Jenny,' said Uncle Paul.

The two fathers tried to wake up their children, but they were both sound asleep, sagging like bags of potatoes on their fathers' shoulders. So, after a short while, Mum and Dad went home with Alexander, while Auntie Susan and Uncle Paul took Jenny home. Katie stayed behind with Grandma and Grandpa.

The firework display was wonderful. Katie held Grandpa's hand when some of the noisier fireworks went off, and waved sparklers around whenever there was a pause. Grandma bought them all hot dogs, and after the display was finished, they went over to the fair, where Katie had a roundabout ride. All too soon, it was time to go home.

'What a pity Alex and Jenny missed the fireworks,' said Katie, as they walked back. 'They'd been looking forward to it such a lot.'

'They were just too tired to stay awake,' said Grandma. 'I think all that noise made everyone tired.'

'I feel tired, as well,' admitted Katie. 'Can noise do that?'

'Noise can do a lot of damage,' said Grandma. 'Shall I tell you a story about noise, on our way home?'

'Yes, please,' said Katie. 'Grandpa, do you think I could have a piggy back ride, please? My feet are worn out.'

So Katie rode up high on Grandpa's shoulders while Grandma told her the story.

'A long time ago,' said Grandma, 'long before Jesus was born, there lived a man called Joshua.'

'Was he a noisy man?' asked Katie. 'There's a Joshua in our class at school, and he's very noisy.'

'No,' said Grandma, 'I expect this Joshua was a quiet man. He would have been quiet so that he could hear God speak to him clearly. One day, Joshua and all of his people were in the desert and they came near to the city of Jericho.

' "You must capture the city of Jericho," said God. But Joshua didn't know how he could do this, because Jericho was protected by a huge strong wall all the way around it.

"I will tell you what to do," said God. He told Joshua that his people must march around the city once a day for six days. They were to blow their trumpets, but nobody was to speak or shout. Joshua explained this to his people, and so they marched around Jericho every day for six days, blowing their trumpets.

'Then, on the seventh day, they went around Jericho seven times, as God had told them to, and on the seventh time, Joshua said to his people, "Now you must all shout, because God has given us this city." So everybody shouted really loudly, and the walls of Jericho fell down flat, and Joshua was able to capture the city.'

'Really,' breathed Katie, who was quite impressed, 'That must have been a surprise for all of the people in the city. But I didn't know that noise could break things.'

'Oh, yes,' said Grandpa. 'For instance, some noises can break glass, and other noises can make people feel very ill. But there's a time for shouting, and a time for being quiet, and God can show us when those times are.'

'Well, I wish that sometimes someone could show Alex when it's time to be quiet,' said Katie.

'Don't forget that he's only a little boy,' said Grandma. 'As he grows up, perhaps you can help to show him when it's time to be quiet.'

By now they had reached Katie's house, and Grandpa knocked on the front door. There was no reply. They waited for a while in the cold, and Grandpa knocked again.

'That's strange,' said Grandma. 'They must be home. I've got my key; I don't expect they'll mind if I let myself in.'

They all went in, and Katie shouted.

'Mummy, we're home!'

There was no answer. They went in to the front room, and there by the fire were Katie's mum and dad, fast asleep.

Grandma laughed quietly.

'I think Alexander's been a bit like Joshua and the walls of Jericho today,' she said. 'He's made so much noise that he's knocked his mum and dad over!'

## Poems

### The wall

The grey stone wall beside my house
Is home to a snail and a darting mouse,
With a frog and a slug and a jumping flea,
They live in perfect harmony.

Where the ancient mortar's crumbled,
And the broken stones lie tumbled,
That's their place to hide away
Until the fading light of day.

Frog hops to the pond to feed,
And wears a hat of emerald weed.
With pulsing throat and staring eyes,
He waits for unsuspecting flies.

Slug and snail go side by side;
Over silvered grass they glide,

Sampling plants so lush and tender,
Ruining the garden's splendour.

Flea, so patient, lies in wait;
With a cat he has a date.
As the tom-cat's voice is raised
So the flea begins to graze.

Small mouse sniffing round the weeds,
Looks for berries, nuts or seeds.
Dry grass makes a comfy nest,
But human hair is still the best.

Beware, my friends who use the wall,
Of cats that prowl or owls that call,
Of herons that parade on stilts,
Of hedgehog, thrush or walls rebuilt.

Until my wall crumbles away,
I will protect you every day.
I'll guard your path round plant and tree,
And hope you never notice me.

## The last sparkler

One last sparkler in the box:
No more sudden, violent shocks
(Designed to rudely keep awake
Hibernating mice and voles)
Of spinning Catherine wheels on poles,
Cracker jacks and thunder flash,
Exploding with a sudden splash
Of smells and colours, smoke and noise.

My last precious sparkler's lit:
Anxiously I watch it spit
Single stars and then a shower;
Stars that fall into the pond,
Bejewel each frog and waving frond.
Sparks sequin the laurel leaves,
Where the garden spider weaves
Diamond-studded gossamer.

Single gems explode and fly,
Splutter, spurt and quickly die.
All too soon the spell is broken;
Just a gnarled and blackened wire,
No more smoke and no more fire.
Secret places turn to dark
With the final mystic spark
Falling on enchanted ground.

## Reading

### *Psalm 150: 3–6*

Praise him with trumpets.
Praise him with harps and lyres.
Praise him with drums and dancing.
Praise him with harps and flutes.
Praise him with cymbals.
Praise him with loud cymbals.
Praise the Lord, all living creatures!
Praise the LORD!

## Prayers

For sparklers and for crackerjacks,
For Catherine wheels that spin and crack,
Bright rockets bursting with the stars,
And noisy 'Rocket ships to Mars',
For bonfire glow and cups of tea,
Hot dogs and fudge and family,
This happy time that Autumn brings,
We thank you God, for everything.

Noise can be; birds singing in a wet garden,
Rain falling on a hot pavement,
Traffic on a busy road,
Pop music on the radio,
Fireworks on a misty Autumn evening,
Crackers at Christmas parties,
Sausages sizzling on a grill.
These sounds are part of your world, God,
And we are thankful if we are able to hear them.

But most important of all is the still, small voice that is your word.
Amen.

## End of Assembly

## Follow-up classwork

Look at animal ears; the obvious ones, such as elephants, hares, dogs and cats, and the less obvious ones, such as frogs, toads and lizards. Find out how snails and worms hear. Make a collection of sounds, using BBC sound effect records. Discuss what we mean by 'Noise'. Make recordings of sounds in your environment. Use them as a background to prose and poetry entitled 'Noise'.

Make paintings using colour and shape to depict musical instruments and the sounds they make.

Make musical instruments using tins, bottles and boxes as drums, shakers and stringed instruments.

## Further reading

**Two Admirals** D. McKee (Andersen Press)
**What Is That Noise?** M. Lemieux (Methuen)

ASSEMBLY 18

# Katie and Goliath

## (David and Goliath)
*1 Samuel 17:1–58*

---

The Katie and Goliath Assembly and story introduce the story of David and Goliath, with its themes of bravery and the confidence that comes with doing God's will. The children can also discuss how difficult it can be to do some things, and how problems can be overcome: how a faith in God can help to overcome our own personal 'Giants'.

## Songs and hymns

**The World is Big, the World is Small** (*33*) Tinder Box (*Black*)
**When a knight won his spurs** (*50*) Come and Praise (*BBC*)

## Read the story

## Katie and Goliath

When Katie came home from school one day, Grandma was there, having a cup of coffee with Katie's mum. Grandma had been there all afternoon, playing with Alexander, and now it was Katie's turn to sit on her lap.

They had a kiss and a cuddle, then Grandma said, 'Tell me about school. Did you have a good time today?'

'Oh, yes,' said Katie, 'I made a gingerbread man. It's in my lunchbox, Mummy.'

Mum took the gingerbread man out of Katie's lunchbox, and showed it to Grandma with a smile. It was huge.

'Mine was the biggest in the class,' said Katie excitedly. 'Mrs Maine said that it was a real gingerbread giant, and later on she told us a story about a giant. Would you like me to tell you the story?'

'Oh, yes, please,' said Grandma.

'Well, it was a long time ago,' said Katie.

'Before Jesus was born?' asked Grandma.

'I think it must have been,' said Katie, 'because Jesus isn't in it. A long time ago there was a boy called David, the same name as David in my class. He was a very small boy.'

'Smaller than Alexander?' asked Grandma.

'No, bigger than that,' said Katie. 'You know, like the big boys at my school. Anyway, an army invaded his country and they had a soldier who was a great big giant. His name was Goliath. He was very very big.'

'Surely not bigger than Grandpa?' interrupted Grandma.

'Yes, of course he was bigger than Grandpa,' snapped Katie, 'I do wish you wouldn't keep interrupting me, Grandma.'

'I'm sorry,' said Grandma, 'but I just wanted to know if he was a big giant or a small giant.'

Katie frowned and looked upwards.

'Look, he was about as high as the ceiling, all right? Now please let me get on or I'll never finish the story.'

'Sorry,' said Grandma meekly.

'Goliath was so big and strong,' went on Katie, 'that he could beat anyone from David's country. Everyone was too scared to fight with Goliath except David. He used to look after some sheep, and he used a sling to throw stones at any wild animals that attacked the sheep. He was very good at that, so he decided to fight Goliath with his sling. Goliath laughed when he saw David coming to fight him, because David was so little. But David threw a stone with his sling and it hit Goliath right in the middle of his forehead and killed him. Then Goliath's army ran away. That's the end of the story.'

'It's a very good story,' said Grandma.

'Mrs Maine said that it means that even if we are very small, we can still be brave, just like David, if we've got difficult things to do.'

'That's quite true,' said Grandma, 'but I've got one question.'

'What's that?' asked Katie.

'When can we taste your gingerbread giant?' said Grandma.

Katie and Alexander had a leg each, Mum and Grandma had an arm each, and the rest was left for Dad when he came home from work.

'Well, that was very tasty,' said Mum, and the others agreed.

Two weeks later, Grandma phoned Katie's mum.

'There's a pantomime at the school down the road,' she said, 'It's Jack and the Beanstalk. Do you think Katie would like to go? I'd be glad to take her.'

'Hold on, I'll ask her,' said Mum.

'What's a pantomime?' asked Katie.

'It's like a play,' said Mum. 'It's called Jack and the Beanstalk.'

'Great,' said Katie, 'I love beans.'

'I don't think she knows that story,' said Mum to Grandma, 'but I think she would love to come.'

'Good,' said Grandma, 'Now, don't tell her the story, or it'll spoil the surprise.'

On the night of the pantomime, Grandma and Grandpa came to collect Katie. She sat in the back seat of their car, strapped in with the seat belt. She had loads of questions to ask. All the way there it was, 'Where will I sit? Can I sit on your lap if I'm frightened? Will there be other children there? Can I take my coat off? Will there be crisps and squash?'

When they reached the school, Katie and Grandma took their seats while Grandpa parked the car. He came to join them later, sitting in the front row with them. There were lots of other children in the front row and they were all very excited, chattering away and rustling sweet papers.

Soon, the music began and everybody went quiet. Katie sat so still that Grandma looked down to see if she'd gone to sleep. She hadn't, but she was sitting spellbound as the curtains parted to show Jack on stage.

Jack told everybody that he'd just sold the cow for a handful of magic beans, and he was going to plant them. The beanstalk grew from the magic beans, and Jack climbed up it to get to the Giant's kingdom. He was hoping to find lots of gold up there.

When the Giant came on stage, Katie got out of her seat. The Giant looked very big in his thick-soled boots and tall hat. Katie turned to Grandma and whispered in a loud voice, 'I know who that is. It's Goliath.'

She watched, open mouthed, as Jack stole the hen that laid golden eggs and climbed down the beanstalk with it. The Giant came back on stage and told the audience just what he was going to do with Jack once he caught him. The audience booed and hissed.

'Oh, no, you're not,' they chanted.

'Oh, yes I am,' replied the Giant.

Katie couldn't contain herself any longer. She jumped right out of her seat and ran up the steps onto the stage.

'Oh, no you're not,' she shouted, 'because I won't let you.'

All the audience went quiet as little Katie stood, hands on hips, in front of the great big Giant. She ran right up to him and gave him a great shove with both hands. Taken by surprise, the Giant toppled over backwards and sat down with a thud.

The audience cheered and clapped and laughed. Little Katie had floored the Giant! Even the Giant laughed as he picked Katie up and tucked her under one arm to carry her back to her seat.

Katie grinned proudly as she climbed up onto Grandpa's lap to watch the rest of the pantomime.

'I like pantomimes,' she whispered to Grandpa.

As they were leaving, Katie said, 'Was I like David?'

'David who?' asked Grandpa.

'You know, David and Goliath,' she replied.

'Oh, yes. Well, a little bit,' said Grandpa with a smile, as they walked to the car.

'That was Mr Smith, anyway,' said Katie, 'It wasn't a real Giant at all, although he is a very big man. He was wearing big boots and a tall hat to make him look like a Giant. Are there any real Giants?'

Grandpa thought for a moment.

'Well, there are some very tall people, but I don't think they're real Giants. And not all Giants would be bad, anyway. I should think that some would be good and some bad, just like ordinary people. Our Giants today are the difficult things that we sometimes have to do. That's when we can show if we are brave like little David was.'

'Or like little Katie was,' put in Grandma with a laugh.

'Was I brave to go on stage?' asked Katie.

'I think you were quite brave,' said Grandpa, 'and just a little bit naughty!'

They all laughed as they drove Katie home.

## Poems

## The Giant

Upon the distant Cotswold Edge,
Where shadow clouds are creeping,
A giant man, alone and lost,
Lies still and softly sleeping.

His tangled hair and rusty beard
Are golden furze and heather;

His smooth stone cheeks are lichen-lined
From mist-hung autumn weather.

His deep, closed eyes are tear dew-ponds;
If dreaming he should sometimes weep.
The mound that is his mighty chest
Is grazed by long-haired nervous sheep.

His moss-green boots lie side by side,
Where primroses and cowslips grow.
His hands hold roots of hawthorn trees
And blackthorn twigs of purple sloe.

His heart beats and he gently sleeps
Beneath his ancient dreaming hill;
Just put your ear close to the earth
And you will hear his breathing still.

## Let's go to the pantomime

Let's go to the pantomime,
To see the magic beanstalk grow,
The genie from Aladdin's Lamp,
And Peter Pan fight his dreaded foe.

Let's go to the pantomime,
To see the horse with rolling eyes.
His tail shoots up and he takes a bow;
He's really two men in disguise.

Let's go to the pantomime,
To see the witch mix her evil brew,
The ugly sisters at the palace ball
And the wicked wolf who was cut in two.

Let's go to the pantomine:
We'll sing and shout and cheer and stamp,
And clap when the hero wins his bride,
And hiss when the baddie takes Aladdin's Lamp.

Let's go to the pantomime!
I'd love to go, please make it soon.

What was that I heard you say?
They don't have pantomimes in June?

## Reading

### *1 Samuel 17:45–47*

David answered,
'You are coming against me with sword, spear, and javelin, but I come against you in the name of the Lord Almighty, the God of the Israelite armies, which you have defied.
This very day the Lord will put you in my power;
I will defeat you and cut off your head . . .
Then the whole world will know that Israel has a God, and everyone here will see that the Lord does not need swords or spears to save his people.

## Prayer

Dear Lord,
Help us to do the things that we don't want to do;
Help us to do the things which are difficult.
With your help, we can do these things,
For you are more powerful than any giant.
Amen

## End of the Assembly

## Follow-up classwork

Goliath was 6 cubits and a span tall; a cubit being about 20" (51 cm) and a span being about 9" (23 cm). Make a large picture of Goliath in chalk on your playground. Measure it in metres and centimetres.

Stick sheets of paper together and draw round the outline of your friends as they lie on it. Now each person can colour or paint inside their own outline. How tall are you? Measure your picture in cubits and spans, metres and centimetres. Display the pictures in order of height.

Make giant gingerbread men.

# Further reading

**Topsy and Tim At the Pantomime** J. & G. Adamson (Blackie)

**The Book of Giant Stories** D. Harrison (Cape)

**The Mysterious Giant of Barletta** T. De Paola (Andersen Press)